Ghost Hunter's Guide
to the San Francisco Bay Area

Ghost Hunter's Guide
to the
San Francisco
Bay Area

By Jeff Dwyer

PELICAN PUBLISHING COMPANY
GRETNA 2005

The word "Pelican" and the depiction of a pelican are trademarks of Pelican Publishing Company, Inc., and are registered in the U.S. Patent and Trademark Office.

Library of Congress Cataloging-in-Publication Data

Dwyer, Jeff.
  Ghost hunter's guide to the San Francisco Bay Area / by Jeff Dwyer.
    p. cm.
  Includes index.
  ISBN 978-1-58980-289-6 (alk. paper)
  1. Ghosts—California—San Francisco Bay Area. 2. Haunted places—California—San Francisco Bay Area. I. Title.
  BF1472.U6D87 2005
  133.1'09794'6—dc22
                                        2004025241

Printed in the United States of America

Published by Pelican Publishing Company, Inc.
1000 Burmaster Street, Gretna, Louisiana 70053

To my children,
Sam, Michael, and Sarah.
May their lives be filled with adventure and wonder.

Table of Contents

Introduction

Who believes in ghosts? People from every religion, culture, and generation believe that ghosts exist. The popularity of ghosts and haunted places in books, televisions programs, and movies reflects the belief of many that other dimensions and spiritual entities exist. In 2000, a Gallup poll discovered a significant increase in the number of Americans who believe in ghosts since the question was first asked in 1978. Thirty-one percent of respondents said they believed ghosts existed. In 1978, only 11 percent admitted to believing in ghosts. Less than a year later, Gallup found that 42 percent of the public believed a house could be haunted but only 28 percent believed we can hear from or mentally communicate with someone who has died. A 2003 Harris poll found as astounding 51 percent of Americans believed in ghosts. As with preceding polls, belief in ghosts was greatest among females. More young people believed in ghosts than older people. Forty-four percent of people aged eighteen to twenty-nine admitted to a belief in ghosts compared with 13 percent of those over sixty-five.

In October, 2001, a major cable television network conducted a survey at its Web site. When asked, "Do you believe in ghosts?" 87 percent of respondents said "Yes!" Fifty-one percent indicated they had seen a ghost but only 38 percent would enter a haunted house alone at night.

Another channel, SciFi, recognized the phenomenal interest of Americans in paranormal activity and launched a weekly, one-hour primetime program on ghost hunting. SciFi also airs programs that investigate psychic abilities, reincarnation, telekinesis, and many other fascinating topics.

Over 56,000 references to ghosts, ghost hunting, haunted places, or related paranormal phenomena were available through the Internet. Clearly, interest in these areas is widespread.

There is no way of knowing how many people have seen or heard a ghost only to feel too embarrassed, foolish, or frightened to admit it. Many ghost hunters and spiritual investigators believe that a vast majority of people have seen or heard something from the other world but failed to recognize it.

The recent world-wide interest in ghosts is not a spin-off of the New Age movement or the current popularity of angels, or the manifestation of some new religious process. The suspicion or recognition that ghosts exist is simply the re-emergence of one of mankind's oldest and most basic beliefs: there is a life after death.

Ancient writings from many cultures describe apparitions and a variety of spirit manifestations that include tolling bells, chimes, disembodied crying or moaning, and whispered messages. Legends and ancient books include descriptions of ghosts, dwelling places of spirits, and periods of intense spiritual activity related to seasons or community events such as festivals or crop harvests.

Vital interactions between the living and deceased have been described as well. Many ancient cultures included dead people, or their spirits, in community life. Spirits of the dead were sought as a source of guidance, wisdom, and protection for the living.

Many believers of the world's oldest religions agree that non-living entities may be contacted for guidance or may be seen on the earthly plane. Among these are visions of saints, the Virgin Mary and angels.

Ancient sites of intense spiritual activity in Arizona, New Mexico, and Central and South America are popular destinations for travelers seeking psychic or spiritual experiences. More modern, local sites, where a variety of paranormal events have occurred, are also popular destinations for adventurous living souls. These ghost hunters seek the spirits of the dearly departed in San Francisco's Victorian mansions and countless other places around the Bay Area ranging from graveyards to the attic of a family home. Modern buildings, bridges, and ships, such as the World War II aircraft carrier USS *Hornet* in Alameda, serve as targets for ghost hunters.

Throughout the past two millennia, the popularity of belief in ghosts has waxed and waned, similar to religious activity. When a rediscovery of ghosts and their role in our lives occurs, skeptics label the notion a fad or an aberration of modern lifestyles. Perhaps people are uncomfortable with the idea that ghosts exist because it involves an examination of our nature and our concepts of life, death, and after-life. These concepts are most often considered in the context of religion, yet ghost hunters recognize that acceptance of the reality of ghosts, and a life after death, is a personal decision, having nothing to do with religious beliefs or church doctrine. An intellectual approach enables the ghost hunter to explore haunted places without religious bias or fears.

The greater frequency of ghostly activities and manifestations in the Bay Area, as evidenced by documentary reports on television and other news media, reflects some people's open-mindedness and widespread interest in ghostly experiences. Ghost hunting is becoming a weekend pastime for many adventurous souls. Advertisement of haunted inns, restaurants, and historical sites is commonplace. It is always fun, often very exciting, and may take ghost hunters places they never dreamed of going.

ABOUT THIS BOOK

Chapter 1 of this book will help you, the ghost hunter, research and organize your own ghost hunt. Chapters 2 through 6 describe several locations at which ghostly activity has been reported. Unlike other collections of ghost stories and descriptions of haunted places, this book emphasizes access. Addresses of each haunted site are included along with other information to assist you in locating and entering the location. Chapter 7 offers organizational material for your ghost hunts, including a checklist of sites and a Sighting Report form to document your adventures. This section also includes lists of suggested reading and videos, and organizations you may contact about your experiences with ghosts.

GHOST HUNTING IN THE BAY AREA

The very word, ghost, immediately brings to mind visions of

ancient European castles, foggy moors, and dark, wind-swept ramparts where brave knights battled enemies of the crown or heroines threw themselves to their death rather than marry the evil duke selected by their noble fathers. The fact is that ghosts are everywhere, and a history based in antiquity, dripping with great sorrow and pain that has persisted for centuries is not essential.

Indeed, the San Francisco Bay Area and its surrounding communities have all the ingredients necessary for successful ghost hunting. The region has been populated for over 200 years with people from a variety of cultures who experienced upheavals, ranging from earthquakes and other disasters of the twentieth century, to the Gold Rush of 1849 and the Spanish Mission period of the early 1800s.

Throughout the Bay Area's history there have been countless opportunities for the spirits of the dearly departed to feel a need to stay on. There are many old buildings, neighborhoods, forts, bar rooms, Spanish missions, wineries, and ships inhabited by ghosts who are often seen or sensed. These lost souls are often the result of violent or unexpected death, often at an early age. These unfortunate people passed with great emotional anguish, leaving their souls with a desire for a completion of their life's objectives, or a sense of obligation to offer protection to a particular place. Some ghosts remain on the earthly plane to provide guidance for someone still alive, or for revenge.

The Bay Area has had its share of criminal activities and social injustice. This has produced many disadvantaged, used, abused, and forlorn people who remain with us after their death. Their souls seek lost dreams while they remain attached to what little they gained during their difficult lives. Many ghosts, harboring resentment, pain, a sense of loss, or a desire to complete their unfinished business, still roam the darkened halls of San Francisco's Victorian mansions, neglected cemeteries, modern buildings, and many other public places throughout the Bay Area.

WHAT IS A GHOST?

The soul leaves the body at the time of death. Its destination is the Other Side. Under some circumstances, some essence of the soul, or spirit, remains on the earthly plane and may be seen or heard as a ghost. Several explanations are offered by spiritualists and scholars of parapsychology as to the nature of these experiences. Many believe that a ghost is a surviving emotional memory or imprint. The emotion, usually associated with a specific place, event, or object, survives because the ghost does not know he is dead, or he cannot accept his new plane of existence. The ghost may be so attached to a thing or a person on the physical plane that he cannot tear himself away in order to move on.

A prominent theory suggests that ghosts may be "psychic ether," derived of mental activity while the person is alive, and existing, or stored, on another plane somewhere between mind and matter. These ethers may be sensed by psychically-sensitive people called *percipients*. Still other theorists suggest that objects absorb psychic impressions, especially those generated by great emotion. The objects then play them back to people who come into contact with the object under the proper conditions. The nature and clarity of the playback, whether visual, auditory or both, depends upon the strength of the emotional imprint and the sensitivity of the percipient.

Others argue that a vehicle or medium, such as an inanimate object, is not necessary. Apparitions may occur in the mind of the percipient resulting from stored psychic images from the past or from transmissions created by the deceased from the other side.

Regardless of which theory is true, it is important to recognize the basic nature of apparitions or ghostly activity. Ghosts are, in most cases, harmless. They do not cause bodily injury nor do they disrupt one's life. Ghosts are not angels, however. It is said that ghosts are the spirits of those who have died, whereas angels are messengers of God.

Ghosts may offer protection, guidance, even comfort, but they may also be mischievous, misleading, angry and revengeful. In this regard, ghosts are not poltergeists. The two major classes of poltergeists are 1) percussive sounds, including raps, thumps, bangs, and crashes, and 2) telekinesis, the movement of inanimate objects including tilting, falling, flying, or hovering.

Poltergeists are usually day-time phenomena focused on a living individual, whereas ghosts prefer nocturnal presentations focused on a place or object. Some authorities argue that poltergeists are person-centered phenomena, resulting from uncontrolled psychic energy within the affected person, rather than the manifestations of an angry or playful ghost.

Finally, ghostly manifestations, or apparitions of sound or visual phenomena, are not considered to be a part of such New Age processes as soul channeling, spiritual possession, or out-of-body experiences. These are person-centered phenomena, whereas ghosts are usually place-bound. They are seen without the aid of spiritual education or media such as trance channelers.

HOW DOES A GHOST MANIFEST ITSELF?

Telekinesis is, perhaps, the most common of ghostly activities. Ghosts like to move or manipulate simple objects such as stacks of coins, playing cards, light switches, or pictures that hang askew. Local temperature changes, such as cold closets, or icy portions of a room, are reported as common. These cold areas are often only a few feet in diameter and they may move about, passing over a ghost hunter.

A thickening of the atmosphere is a common occurrence prior to the appearance of a ghost. The sensation has been described as though a small room suddenly became crowded with many people. Some people believe that sounds and odors are coincidental with a ghost's presence. For example, screams or moans are associated with the ghost's violent death while odors may reflect his experience of languishing in prison or burning in a fire. Odors of tobacco, oranges, and hemp are commonly reported. Humanoid images are the prized objective of most ghost hunters but they are the least to be experienced. When such images appear, they are often partial, revealing a head and torso with an arm or two.

Full body apparitions are rare. The solidity of these images is highly variable. Some hunters have seen ethereal, fully transparent forms that are barely discernible while others describe ghosts that appear as solid as a living being. While remaining invisible to the human eye, some ghosts prefer to manifest themselves on photographic film. The Polaroid camera's film medium gives the ghost hunter immediate evidence of activity.

IS GHOST HUNTING DANGEROUS?

Ghost hunting is not dangerous. Motion pictures and children's ghost stories have created a widespread notion that ghosts may inflict harm or even cause the death of persons they dislike. There are only a few reliable reports of ghosts attacking people, however. Persons who claim to have been injured by a ghost have, in most cases, precipitated the injury themselves through their own ignorance or fear. The ghost of the Abbot of Trondheim was reputed to have attacked some people decades ago, but circumstances and precipitating events are unclear. Authorities believe that rare attacks by ghosts are a matter of mistaken identity, i.e., the ghost missidentified a living person as a figure known to the ghost from his life.

It is possible that attacks may be nothing more than clumsy efforts by a ghost to achieve recognition. Witnesses of ghost appearances have found themselves in the middle of gun-fights, major military battles, and other violent events yet sustained not the slightest injury. If the ghost hunter keeps a wary eye and a calm attitude, and sets aside tendencies to fear the ghost or the circumstances of its appearance, he will be safe.

Most authorities agree that ghosts do not travel. Ghosts will not follow you home, take up residence in your car, or attempt to occupy your body. They are held in a time and space by deep emotional ties to an event or place. Ghosts have been observed on airplanes, trains, buses, and ships, however. It is unlikely that the destination interests them. Something about the journey, some event such as a plane crash or train wreck, accounts for their appearance as travelers.

UNDER WHAT CONDITIONS IS A SIGHTING MOST LIKELY?

Although ghosts may appear at any time, a sighting may occur on special holidays, anniversaries (July 4, December 7), birthdays, or during historic periods, or calendar periods pertaining to the personal history or emotional anguish of the ghost. Halloween is reputed to be a favorite night for many apparitions, while others seem to prefer their own special day, or night, on a weekly or monthly cycle.

Night is a traditional time for ghost activity, yet experienced ghost hunters know that sightings may occur at any time. There seems to be no consistent affinity of ghosts for darkness, but they seldom appear when artificial light is bright. Perhaps this is why ghosts shy away from camera crews and their array of lights. Ghosts seem to prefer peace and quiet although some of them have been reported to make incessant, loud sounds. Even a small group of ghost hunters may make too much sound to facilitate a sighting. For this reason, it is recommended that a group be limited to four persons and oral communication be kept to a minimum.

WHY DO GHOSTS REMAIN IN A PARTICULAR PLACE?

Ghosts remain in a particular place because they are emotionally attached to a room, a building, activities, events, or special surroundings that profoundly affected them during their lives or played a role in their death. A prime example is the haunted house, inhabited by the ghost of a man who hung himself in the master bedroom because his wife left him. It is widely believed that a ghost is confused by his death and the sudden transition from the physical world. He or she remains in familiar or emotionally stabilizing surroundings to ease the strain. A place-bound ghost is most likely to occur when a violent death occurred with great emotional anguish. Ghosts may linger in a house, barn, cemetery, factory, or store waiting for a loved one or anyone familiar who might help them deal with their new level of existence. Some ghosts wander through buildings or forests, on bridges, or alongside particular sections of roads. Some await enemies and seek revenge. Some others await a friend and a chance for resolution of their guilt.

HOT SPOTS FOR GHOSTLY ACTIVITY

Numerous disasters, areas of criminal activity, and locations of other tragic events abound in the San Francisco Bay Area providing hundreds of sites for ghost hunting. You may visit primary locations described in chapters 2 through 6 to experience ghostly activity discovered by others, or discover a hot spot to research and initiate your own ghost hunt.

The Bay Area's bridges have been the venue selected by many suicidal persons to end their life in a tragic and dramatic fashion. The Golden Gate Bridge is well-known throughout the world as a jumper's choice. Over six hundred known suicides have occurred at the Golden Gate Bridge, usually mid-span facing San Francisco Bay. The San Francisco-Oakland Bay Bridge is less famous as a vehicle for suicide but it has been the locale selected by several jumpers and the site of several fatal accidents. Its most recent notoriety arose at the time of the 1989 Loma Prieta earthquake when a section of the upper road-bed collapsed at the Oakland end of the bridge, killing two people.

Earthquakes have resulted in a large number of sudden and tragic deaths in the Bay Area. The San Francisco earthquake and fire of April 17, 1906, killed over three thousand persons and destroyed the homes of many others who, dying in later years, could never let go of their memories of a cherished house or favorite site within the old city.

On October 17, 1989, the Loma Prieta earthquake killed sixty people on the I-80 Cypress Freeway in Oakland when that stretch of elevated road-bed collapsed. That portion of the freeway was not rebuilt. The site is occupied by a surface street named in honor of Dr. Martin Luther King, Jr.

The Marina District of San Francisco was the site of several deaths from the earthquake of 1989 due to the collapse of many buildings and the fires that followed. The devastation is quite apparent in many structures that remain only partially rebuilt.

The Bay Area's most recent major disaster occurred in the Oakland hills on October 21, 1992, when a fire storm destroyed thousands of homes and killed eighty-three desperate people as they raced ahead of the flames and suffocating smoke, trying to escape.

Many adobe missions exist throughout the Bay Area dating from the early 1800s. Most of them are well-preserved and open to the public. The grounds of these monuments to California's Spanish Period comprise mass burial sites for thousands of Indians, many of whom lost their culture, language, religion, and freedom under the harsh rule of Spain and the mission fathers. Mission Dolores in San Francisco, Mission San Jose in Fremont, and Mission Solano in Sonoma possess fascinating histories and an ambience conducive to ghost hunting.

The homes of many Bay Area pioneers, such as General Vallejo's home in Sonoma, and the George Yount mansion in the Napa Valley, are reputed to be the residence of ghosts. Of course, San Jose has the world-famous Winchester Mystery House while Oakland, Alameda, and some towns in Marin County have many Victorian mansions with curious histories and ghostly atmospheres. Some of these charming old homes have become bed-and-breakfast inns and exciting weekend destinations for ghost hunters.

The Army Presidio of San Francisco was founded in 1769 by Spanish explorers but is best known as an American military base. It encompasses several buildings constructed before the Civil War, and numerous camp-sites used by soldiers prior to shipping out for the battlefields of the Civil War, Spanish-American War, World Wars I and II, Korea, and Vietnam. Many of these sites, and the darkened hallways of the older buildings, hold the essence of days long passed and, perhaps, the spirits of some of those old soldiers.

The Presidio's Crissy Field—now a waterfront recreation area—was the headquarters of the Ninth Aero Squadron during World War I. Some of the squadron's brave pilots, flying rickety, unstable biplanes in rough winds gusting through the nearby Golden Gate, died tragic and untimely deaths on the landing field.

Visible from Crissy Field is Fort Point, situated under the south ramp to the Golden Gate Bridge. Fort Point was a military establishment, bristling with canon to protect the Golden Gate. The Army Corps of Engineers built the fort of brick in 1856. A young officer named Robert E. Lee was a member of the corps. Cold, dark passageways echo the sounds of passing ships and sometimes a passing ghost or two.

Nineteenth-century cemeteries are scattered about the Bay Area, many of them quite small and tucked away in seldom-visited areas with unattended graves and forgotten decedents. Sonoma, Los Gatos, Oakland, and San Jose have cemeteries that contain the remains of particularly interesting people, including criminals and pioneers.

One of the most fascinating haunted sites in the Bay Area is the Federal prison on Alcatraz Island, home to prisoners often referred to as the living dead, such as Robert Stroud, the bird-man of Alcatraz. The island prison is accessible by tour boat from San Francisco's Fisherman's Wharf. Its ghosts have been featured on several television programs.

Astute ghost hunters often search historical maps and other documents to find the sites of old buildings now occupied by modern structures. The former site of the Niantic Hotel in San Francisco is one such place. The Niantic was a sailing vessel that arrived in the Bay during the Gold Rush of 1849. Like so many other sailing vessels, she was abandoned by her crew who dashed off to the Sierra Nevada in search of gold. The derelict ship was run aground and turned into a boarding house. Over the years, land was filled around the Niantic and she was absorbed into the growing city as an odd but well-patronized hotel for the riotous clientele of the city's Barbary Coast.

The Niantic Hotel literally sank into the unstable soil of San Francisco's expanding coastline and became the foundation of more modern structures. Historians estimate that the Niantic Hotel and, perhaps, some of its patrons, lies somewhere along Battery Street.

Across the street from the Holiday Inn at San Francisco's Fisherman's wharf is a small triangular plot of ground that serves as the final resting-place for the stern section of another vessel, swallowed up by the fast growing city in the 1850s. Many interesting artifacts were found in the hull when it was unearthed during construction of the inn, but the fate of her crew remains a mystery.

TECHNICAL AIDS

For over a hundred years, investigators have tried to record irrefutable evidence of ghostly activity. The practice of "spirit photography," started in 1861, has regained popularity many times in the twentieth century only to elicit accusations of fraud. Genuine images of ghosts on film are rare, but it is a worthwhile endeavor and fun.

Audio recordings of ghosts were attempted soon after Thomas Edison invented the dictaphone. In the late 1950s and throughout the 1960s, the recording of spectral sounds was a popular and primary means of investigating the other world. Sounds, as with visual presentations, are often vague and open to broad interpretation. Those that are clear, with logical and verifiable messages, are most often labeled a fraud. See chapter 1 for a discussion of audio and photographic techniques.

Games, toys, and obstacles can be useful indicators of ghost activity, aside from technical approaches that often involve expensive audio or video recording equipment.

Ghosts seem unable to resist an opportunity to manipulate simple objects left in their path, especially those that provide them with an opportunity to announce their presence and interact with the physical world. We recommend that you leave a stack of pennies, five to ten, at the site over night. They may be scattered in the morning. Also, leave a deck of cards with four aces at the top. Your ghost may rearrange the deck.

As a rule, ghosts cannot tolerate disturbances within the place they haunt. If you tilt a wall-mounted picture, the ghost will set it straight. Obstacles placed in a ghost's path may be pushed aside. Leave a book leaning against a door, then leave the room for a few hours. The book may be toppled when you return. Leave an object on a ghost's grave, chair, or any other place dear to the spirit, and you may find it moved within minutes.

Ghosts seem to enjoy making patterns with matchsticks. Moving or hiding keys, turning off lights, and turning door knobs. These seemingly minor indications of ghostly activity should be recorded on the sighting report form in Appendix A.

Two general rules apply for successful ghost hunting. The first is to be patient. Ghosts are everywhere, but contact may require a considerable investment of time. The second rule is to have fun.

You may report your ghost hunting experiences or suggest hot spots for ghost hunting to the author by visiting the Web site www.ghostreport.com.

Ghost Hunter's Guide
to the San Francisco Bay Area

CHAPTER 1

How to Hunt for Ghosts

You may visit recognized haunted sites, listed in chapters 2 through 6, using some of the ghost hunting techniques described later in this chapter, or you can conduct your own spirit investigation. If that is the case, chose a place you think might be haunted, like an old house in your neighborhood or a favorite Victorian bed-and-breakfast inn. You may get a lead from fascinating stories about ancestors that have been passed down through your family.

Your search for a ghost, or exploration of a haunted place, starts with research. Summaries of obscure and esoteric material about possible haunted sites are available from museums, local historical societies, and bookstores. Brochures and booklets, sold at historical sites under the California State Park system, can be good resources, too.

Guided tours of historical sites such as Monterey's historical buildings, the Winchester Mystery House in San Jose, Spanish missions in San Francisco and San Rafael, or Alcatraz prison are good places to begin your research. Touring buildings can help you develop a feel for places within a building where ghosts might be.

In addition, touring haunted buildings offers you an opportunity to speak with guides and docents who may be able to provide you with clues about the dearly departed or tell you ghost stories you can't find in published material. Docents may know people—old timers in the area or amateur historians—who can give you additional information about a site, its former owners or residents, and its potential for ghostly activity.

Almost every city has a local historical society (See Appendix G). These are good places to find information that may not be published anywhere else, such as histories of local families and buildings, information about tragedies, disasters, criminal activity, or legends and myths about places that may be haunted. You will want to takes notes about secret scandals or other ghost-producing happenings that occurred at sites before survivors built modern buildings. In these cases, someone living in a new house could hear strange sounds, feel cold spots, or see ghosts.

Newspapers are an excellent source of historical information as well. You can view stories from old issues via the Internet. Or you can access the newspaper's Web site and look up either dates or topics such as haunted houses or ghosts. Newspaper files about suicides, murders, train wrecks, plane crashes, and reports of paranormal phenomena can often provide information for your research. Stories about authentic haunted sites are common around Halloween.

Bookstores and libraries usually have special interest sections with books on local history by local writers. A few inquiries may connect you with these local writers, who may be able to help you focus your research.

If these living souls cannot help, try the dead. A visit to a local graveyard is always fruitful in identifying possible ghosts. Often you can find headstones that indicate the person entombed died of suicide, criminal activity, local disaster, or such. Some epitaphs may indicate if the deceased was survived by a spouse and children, or died far from home.

Once you have a name and date of death, you have enough information to begin you search for ghostly activity.

Perhaps the best place to start a search for a ghost is within your own family. Oral histories can spark your interest in a particular ancestor, scandal, building, or site relevant to your family. Old photographs, death certificates, letters, wills, anniversary lists in family Bibles, and keepsakes can be great clues. Then you can visit gravesites and/or homes of your ancestors to check out the vibes as you mentally and emotionally empathize with specific aspects of your family's history.

Almost every family has a departed member who died at an early age, suffered hardships and emotional anguish, passed away suddenly due to an accident or natural disaster, or was labeled a skeleton in the family's closet. Once you have focused your research on a deceased person, you need to determine if that person remains on this earthly plane as a ghost.

Evaluate the individual's personal history to see if he had a reason to remain attached to a specific place. Ask the following questions:

Was his death violent or under tragic circumstances?

Did he die at a young age with unfinished business?

Did the deceased leave behind loved ones who needed his support and protection?

Was this person attached to a specific site or building?

Would the individual be inclined to seek revenge against those responsible for his death?

Would his devotion and sense of loyalty lead him to offer eternal companionship to loved ones?

Revenge, anger, refusal to recognize the reality of transformation by death, and other negative factors prompt many spirits to haunt places and people. However, most ghosts are motivated by positive factors. Spirits may remain at a site to offer protection or they had a great love for a particular place.

Also, remember that ghosts can appear as animals or objects. Apparitions of ships, buildings, covered wagons, bridges, and roads by the strictest definitions, are phantoms, the essence of a structure that no longer exists on the physical plane. There are many reports of houses, cottages, even villages and ships, that were destroyed or sunk years before.

BASIC PREPARATION FOR GHOST HUNTING

If you decide to ghost hunt at night, or on a special anniversary, make a trip to the site a few days ahead of time. During daylight hours, familiarize yourself with the place and its surroundings. Many historical sites are closed after sunset or crowded at certain times by organized tours.

EQUIPMENT PREPARATION

A few days before your ghost hunt, purchase fresh film for your camera and audio recording devices. Test your batteries and bring back-up batteries and power-packs with you. You should have two types of flashlights: a broad-beam light for moving around a site, and a penlight-type flashlight for narrow-field illumination while you make notes or adjust equipment. A candle is a good way to light the site because it is probably the least offensive to your ghost.

STILL-PHOTOGRAPHY TECHNIQUES

Many photographic techniques that work well under normal conditions are inadequate for ghost hunts. That's because ghost hunting is usually conducted under conditions of low, ambient light requiring long exposures. Some investigators use a strobe or flash device but they can make the photos look unauthentic.

Practice taking photographs with films of various light sensitivities before you go on your ghost hunt. Standard photographic films of high light sensitivity should be used—ASA of 800 or higher is recommended. At a dark or nearly-dark location, mount the camera on a tripod. Try several exposure settings from one to thirty seconds, and aperture settings under various low-light conditions.

Make notes about the camera settings that work best under various light conditions. Avoid aiming the camera at a scene where there is a bright light such as a street lamp or exit sign over a doorway. These light sources may "over-flow" throughout your photograph.

Some professional ghost hunters use infrared film. You should consult a professional photo lab technician about this type of film and its associated photographic techniques. Several amateur ghost hunters use Polaroid-type cameras with interesting results. The rapid film developing system of these cameras give almost instant feedback about your technique and/or success in documenting ghost activities. Ghosts have reportedly written messages on Polaroid film.

Many digital cameras have features that enable automatic exposures at specific intervals, e.g., once every minute. This allows a "hands-off" remote photograph record to be made. Repetitive automatic exposures also allow a site to be investigated without the presence of the investigator.

Your equipment should include a steady, light-weight tripod. Hand-held cameras tend to produce poorly focused photographs when the exposure duration is greater than $\frac{1}{60}$ second.

AUDIO RECORDING TECHNIQUES

Tape recorders provide an inexpensive way to obtain evidence of ghostly activity. Always test your recorder under conditions you expect to find at the investigation site.

Does your recorder pick-up excessive background noise? This may obscure ghostly sounds. If so, consider up-grading the tape quality as high as possible and use a microphone with a wind guard.

Use two or more recorders at different locations within the site. This allows you to verify sounds such as wind against a window and reduce the possibility of ambiguous recordings.

You can use sound-activated recorders at a site over night. They will automatically switch on whenever a sound occurs above a minimum threshold. Be aware that each sound on the tape will start with an annoying wowing artifact, the result of a slow tape speed at the beginning of each recorded segment. The slow tape speed could obscure the sounds made by a ghost.

Remote microphones and monitor earphones allow you to remain some distance from the site and activate the recorder when ghostly sounds are heard. If this equipment is not available, use long-play tape (sixty to ninety minutes), turn the recorder on, and let it run throughout your hunt, whether you remain stationary or walk about the site. This will provide you with a means of making audio notes rather than written notes. A head set with a microphone is especially useful with this technique.

VIDEO RECORDING

Video recorders offer a wide variety of recording features from time-lapse to auto-start/stop, and auto-focus. These features enable you to make surveillance-type recordings over many hours while you are off-site. Consult your user's manual for low-light recording guidelines and always use a tripod and long-duration battery packs.

If you plan to attempt video recording, consider using two recorders, at equal distance from a specific object such as a chair. Arrange the recorders at different angles, preferably 90 degrees from the object on which both are focused.

Another approach you might try is to use a wide-angle setting on camera number one, to get a broad view of a room, porch, or court-yard. On camera number two, use a long-focal length setting to produce a close-up of a chair, window, or door that may be a site for ghostly apparitions.

You may have great success with continuous play techniques rather than sequential, manual, or timer-actuated tape runs. If you try this last technique, use tape runs of one to five minutes. Practice with the method that interrupts the automatic setting should you need to manually control the recording process. Always use a tripod that can be moved to a new location in a hurry.

HIGH TECH EQUIPMENT

Night vision goggles can be useful in low-light situations. You can see doors, curtains, and other objects move that you might not otherwise see. These goggles are quite expensive, however.

You can buy electromagnetic field detectors, as well as motion detectors, at your local electronics store or over the Internet. Unless you have a means of recording the output, your reports of anomalies, movement and apparitions will not be the kind of hard evidence you need for the skeptics.

OTHER EQUIPMENT

Various authorities in the field of ghost hunting suggest the following items to help you mark sites, detect paranormal phenomena, and collect evidence of ghostly activity.

White/colored chalk	Small mirror
Compass	Small bell
Stop watch	Plastic bags for evidence
Steel tape measure	Matches
Magnifying glass	Tape for sealing doors
First aid kit	String
Thermometer	A cross
Metal detector	Bible
Graph paper for diagrams	Cell phone

GROUP ORGANIZATION AND PREPARATION

It is not necessary to be a believer in spirits or paranormal phenomena in order to see a ghost or experience haunting activities. Indeed, most reports of ghost activities are made by unsuspecting people who never gave the matter much thought.

You should not include people in your group with openly negative attitudes about these things. If you include skeptics, be sure they maintain an open mind and are willing to participate in a positive group attitude. You may find the meditation techniques useful, described later in this chapter, in achieving an optimal level of sensitivity.

Keep your group small, limited to four members if possible. Ghosts have been seen by large groups, but small groups are more easily managed and likely to be of one mind in terms of objectives and methods.

Meet an hour or more prior to starting the ghost hunt at a location away from the site. Review the history of the ghost you seek and the previous reports of ghost activity at the site. Discuss the group's expectations based on known or suspected ghostly activity or specific research goals. Review audio and visual apparitions, telekinesis, local temperature changes, and intended methods of identifying or recording these phenomena. Most importantly, agree to a plan of action if a sighting is made by any member of the group.

The first priority for a ghost hunter is to maintain visual or auditory contact without a lot of activity such as making notes. Without breaking contact, do the following:

- activate recording devices
- redirect audio, video, or photographic equipment to focus on the ghost
- move yourself to the most advantageous position for listening or viewing the ghostly activity
- attract the attention of group members with a code-word, hand signal (touch the top of your head), or any action that signals other hunters so they can pick-up your focus of attention

Should you attempt to interact with the ghost? Only if the ghost invites you to speak or move. Often, ghost hunter's movement or noise frightens the ghost, or interferes with the perception of the apparition.

MEDITATION

You may experience ghost activities without prior knowledge of the ghost, his personal history, or the haunted place. Your religious affiliation or beliefs are irrelevant. Often, psychological or emotional preparation, research, or special equipment is not essential.

Many sightings have been serendipitous and quite a surprise to the percipient. Some ghost hunters cite two factors that may increase the possibility of seeing a ghost: the emotional imprint or attachment of the deceased to a particular place, and the degree of sympathy or sensitivity the percipient has for the ghost. The first factor may be revealed by research while the second is a matter of personal psychological preparation or attitude adjustment.

Ghost hunters can prepare themselves for experiencing a ghost by being sympathetic toward the ghost or his tragic history, or by having empathy for the ghost's emotional entrapment on the earthly plane. To do this you need to open your mind to the reality of ghosts and try to understand the ghost's emotional predicament.

If you go on a ghost hunt with a group, all of the members need to be of one mind in this regard. Someone with a skeptical attitude or intense negative belief toward ghosts will block the other ghost hunters' perception of ghost activity. The ghost will feel the unwelcome attitude and stay quiet and out of view.

This leads to another factor—meditation, the simple process of relaxing one's physical body to eliminate distracting thoughts and tensions. When you meditate you focus your spiritual awareness and physical mind on a single subject. The objective is to connect with your highest, innermost self. That way you can open your mind and spiritual awareness to the world around you. The process enables you to mentally disregard worries, negative thoughts, and attitudes that may interfere with your concentration on the ghost you seek. Meditation increases your sensitivity and focus. Keep in mind that it is possible to be in a meditation "state" and still function while appearing quite normal.

When you arrive at the site of your ghost hunt, find a place a short distance away to meditate. Three essentials for any effective meditation are comfort, quiet, and concentration.

Comfort: Sit or stand in a relaxed position. Take free and even breaths at a slow rate. Do not alter your breathing pattern so much that you feel short-of-breath, winded, or lightheaded. Close your eyes, if that enhances your comfort. Or focus on a candle, a tree, or a flower. Do not fall asleep. Proper meditation creates relaxation without decreasing alertness.

Quiet: Meditate in a place away from noises generated by traffic, passersby, radios, slamming doors, and the like. If you are with a group, give each other sufficient personal space. Some people use mantras, repetitive words or phrases, or speak only in their mind in order to facilitate inner calmness.

Mantras are useful to induce a focused state of relaxation but they may disrupt the meditation of a companion if spoken aloud. A majority of ghost hunters do not believe that mantras are necessary in this instance. They point out that ghost hunting is not like a séance as depicted in old movies.

It is not necessary to chant special words, call out to the dead, or invite an appearance "from beyond the grave."

Concentration: First, you want to clear your mind of everyday thoughts, worries, and concerns. This is the most difficult part of the process. Many of us don't want to let go of our stressful thoughts. To help you let go of those thoughts, let the thought turn off its light and fade into darkness. After you clear your mind, some thoughts may reappear. Repeat the process. Slowly turn off the light of each thought until you can rest with a completely cleared mind. This might take some practice. Don't wait until you are on the scene of a ghost hunt before you practice this exercise.

Once your mind is clear, focus on your breathing as you imagine your entire being at a single point of energy driving the breathing process. Then, open yourself—think only of the entity you seek. Expand your focus on his identity (if known), history, reported nature and appearance, or activity.

Mentally look at each thought as you continue relaxed breathing.

Find a thought that is most attractive to you, then expand your mind to include your present surroundings. Return slowly to your current place and time. Remain quiet for a minute or two before you resume communication with your companions and move ahead with the ghost hunt.

SEARCHING FOR GHOSTS

There are no strict rules or guidelines for successful ghost hunting except to be patient! Professional ghost hunters sometimes wait several days, weeks, and even months before achieving contact with a ghost. Others have observed full-body apparitions when they least expected it, while concentrating fully on some other activity. Regardless of the depth of your research or preparation, you need to be patient. The serious ghost hunter will anticipate that several trips to a haunted site may be required before some sign of ghostly activity is observed.

If you hunt with a group, you need to establish a communications system in the event that even one member might sight a ghost or experiences some evidence of ghostly activity. Of course, confirmation by a second person is important in establishing validity and credibility. A hand signal (like touching your hand to the top of your head) was recommended as a means of informing others that they should direct their eyes and ears to a site indicated by the person in contact with a ghost. Because of this, all ghost hunters need to keep their companions in sight at all times and be aware of hand signals.

An audio signal can often reduce the need for monitoring other ghost hunters for hand signals. It is equally important for a group to establish a method for calling other hunters who may be some distance away. Tugging on a length of string can be an effective signal. So can beeping devices, mechanical "crickets," and flashing penlight signals, i.e., one flash for a cold spot and two flashes for an apparition. Hand-held radios, or walkie-talkies, can also be effective. Some models can send audio signals or activate flashing lights. Cell phones can be used but the electromagnetic activity may be uninviting to your ghost.

Remaining stationary within a room, a gravesite, courtyard, or other confirmed location is often most productive. If a ghost is known to have a favorite chair, window, or other place within a room, he will appear. Under these conditions, the patient ghost hunter will have a successful hunt.

If your ghost does not have a favorite place within a room or outdoor area, position yourself to gain the broadest view of the site. A corner of a room is optimal because it allows the ghost unobstructed motion about the place while avoiding the impression of a trap set by uninvited people who occupy his favorite space. If you are outdoors at a gravesite, for instance, position yourself at the base of a tree or in the shadows of a monument to conceal your presence while affording a view of your ghost's grave.

If your ghost is a mobile spirit, moving throughout a house, over a bridge, or about a courtyard or graveyard, you may have no choice but to move around the area. Search for a place where you feel a change in the thickness of the air, or a cold spot, or a peculiar odor.

If you are ghost hunting with others, it may be advantageous to station members of your group at various places in the ghost's haunting grounds and use a reliable system to alert others to spirit activity. Each member could then patrol a portion of the site. Radio or cell phone communications may be essential for this type of ghost hunt.

Once you are on site, the above-described meditation may help you focus and maintain empathy for your ghost. Investigate sounds, even common sounds, as the ghost attempts to communicate with you. Make mental notes of the room temperature, air movement, and the sensations of abrupt change in atmosphere as you move about the site. Changes in these factors may indicate the presence of a ghost.

Pay attention to your own sensations or perceptions, such as the odd feeling that someone is watching you or standing close by. Your ghost may be hunting you! Sensations of pressure on you shoulder or other body parts may be the hand of a ghost.

WHAT TO DO WITH A GHOST

On occasion, professional ghost hunters make contact with a ghost by entering a trance and establishing two-way communications. The ghost hunter speaks to the ghost so their companions can hear what he says, but the ghost's voice can only be heard by the trance communicator. Sylvia Brown's book, *Adventures of a Psychic,* describes several of these trance communication sessions. However, most ghost encounters are brief and limited to telekinesis or audio activity with no opportunity to speak to the ghost.

Amateur ghost hunters, and those who happen to encounter a ghost, are often content to experience whatever visual, auditory, or telekinetic activity the ghost wishes to present. Actual conversations are rare and often suspect, but the ghost may make gestures or acknowledge the person's presence through eye contact, a touch on the shoulder, sound, or a movement.

The ghost hunter must decide to follow the gestures or direction of a ghost or not. A lady ghost in the Gold Rush country stands at the roadside, beckoning motorists to turn into the Pioneer Cemetery for a visit! To date, none of the visitors who accepted her invitation have suffered ill effects.

Invitations, such as this, are frightening to most of us. More often, the ghost's activities are directed at getting the intruder to leave a room, house, or gravesite. If you sense your ghost wants you to leave, most hunters believe it is best not to push one's luck. When you have established the nature of the ghost activity, ascertained that your companions have experienced the activity, made a few photographs and run a few minutes of audiotape, it may be time to leave. An experience with an unfriendly ghost can often lead to nightmares.

Residents of haunted houses and employees of haunted business establishments often accept the ghost's telekinetic or audio activities without concern. It is part of the charm of a place and may add some fun.

AFTER THE GHOST HUNT

Turn off all recorders and move them to a safe place. Some ghost hunters suspect that ghosts can erase tapes. Label your tapes with the date, time, and location. Use a code number for each tape. Keep a separate record of the where the tape was made, date, time, and contents. Place tapes in a waterproof bag with your name, address, telephone number, and a note that guarantees postage in case it is misplaced.

Have photographic film developed at a professional color laboratory. Professionals at the lab may help you with special enhancement and cropping. Have copies made of the negatives that contain ghostly images.

All members of the group should meet right after the hunt, away from the site. Each hunter who witnessed ghostly activity or an apparition should make a written or audio statement describing the experience. The form presented in Appendix B is for the group leader to complete. Video and audio recordings made at the site should be reviewed and reconciled with witness statements. Then, plans should be made for a follow-up visit in the near future to the site to confirm the apparition, its nature and form, and the impressions and experiences of the initial ghost hunt.

Data about the ghost's location within a site, time of day or night, phase of the moon, season, degree and size of cold spots, as well as form and density of an apparition, may indicate the optimal conditions for future contact with a ghost. Patience and detailed records can help you to achieve the greatest reward for a ghost hunter—unmistakable proof of ghostly activity.

CHAPTER 2

North Bay Area

The North Bay area has been for years the quiet part of the Bay Area. Much of the land in this region is devoted to agriculture, primarily wine grapes, and there are no large cities comparable to San Jose, Oakland, or San Francisco. The history of the region is enriched with preserved Spanish Missions, quaint villages, lonely stretches of country roads, quiet beaches, and several old wineries. The I-80 corridor, traversing the northeast portion of this region, passes through many old towns as it heads to historic Sacramento and the Gold Rush country.

THE GHOST OF 3 WEST

Kaiser Foundation Medical Center
Rehabilitation Division
975 Sereno Drive
Vallejo, CA 94589
(707) 651-2360 (Hospital Volunteer's Information desk)

Kaiser Medical Center was constructed over the former site of the old county hospital. The county hospital sat on the site of a military recuperation hospital used extensively during World War II. Soldiers, sailors, and flyers were brought there from military hospitals throughout the Pacific for long-term rest and rehabilitation from injuries received in combat. The old wooden barracks were converted for use as a county hospital in 1947. Early in 1960 they were torn down and replaced with the Kaiser Medical Center. Reportedly, the space currently occupied by a ward designated "3 West" is directly over the portion of the old military hospital where several servicemen suffered many months before dying from battlefield wounds.

The ghost of 3 West has been described as a young man dressed in a bomber-style leather jacket. He is seen primarily by housekeeping staff in the late evening or early morning hours. His special place is on the third floor of the rehab medical center but he has been seen wandering the adjacent wing that houses offices and treatment rooms for various rehabilitation services.

This ghost is manifested through telekinesis. He manipulates light switches and doors and has been known to move cleaning equipment several feet as if he were playing a game. It is possible that he did not want the equipment sitting in a place "occupied" by a friend or a spot significant to his own illness or death. Most recently, this ghost has been turning a secretary's clock ahead by one hour each day.

His presence is manifest by a thickening of the atmosphere and cold spots. Several staff members have reported a chilling feeling that someone is watching them as they work at a computer.

Few people have actually seen this ghost, but his partial apparition has been seen as he moves around corners. He appears so real that staff members chase after him, thinking he is a visitor in violation of visiting hours. Upon turning the corner, nothing but deserted hallways lay before the puzzled staff. This ghost seldom appears during midday hours, although late one morning a woman watched in amazement as a depression in a vinyl seat returned to a more rounded shape as though a person sitting there rose to his feet.

Many electrical problems have been encountered on 3 West. New electrical circuits were installed on that floor in an attempt to resolve power surges, lighting failures, and other phenomenon for which no apparent cause was discovered. Members of the staff are so unnerved by this ghost that they leave lights on in rooms not occupied by patients as they go about their late-night housekeeping duties.

A list of the number of service men treated at the old military hospital and barracks is no longer available. It is unlikely that we will ever learn the name of this ghost, his personal history, or his reason for remaining at 3 West.

Some staff members suspect there are several ghosts here. In the outpatient physical therapy clinic, the odor of cigar smoke is often sensed although smoking is banned throughout the entire facility. At least two apparitions have been seen in the ICU. Nurses report an elderly woman dressed in black and the apparition of a patient who died after several weeks in the ICU bed.

MISSION SAN FRANCISCO SOLANO

100 East Spain Street
Sonoma, CA 95476
(707) 938-1519 (State Historical Park Headquarters)

On the northeast corner of Sonoma's town plaza sits the last of the missions established by the Spanish in their quest to colonize California. The Catholic Church played a leading role in the process of settling the region, sending priests to establish a long chain of

Mission San Francisco Solano, located in Sonoma, is surrounded by unmarked graves of Indians and early-California pioneers.

missions, each separated by one day's travel on horseback, from the Mexican border to the frontier of northern California. Their principle objective was to convert the local American Indians to Catholicism and the Spanish way of life. It was believed that this would create a peaceful, subservient population loyal to the Church and the crown of Spain. Such a population would enable the development of secular interests that included taking land from the natives and using them as slave labor. This process destroyed native religions, social traditions, and small Indian communities while robbing natives of their land and cultural identity.

Mission Solano was founded by Father Jose Altimira and consecrated July 4, 1823. As construction of additional structures continued in 1824 through 1825, friction developed between Father Altimira and local Indians, who were pressed into service as slave laborers. By all accounts, mission life was harsh and often cruel. Punishment was dispensed for failure to learn Spanish, religious lessons, and cultural traditions of the mission fathers.

Finally, in 1826, the Indians drove the demanding priest and other mission fathers out of Sonoma. With the reestablishment of amicable relations through the intervention of Father Fortuni, the mission Indian population grew to almost one thousand by 1830. By 1846, however, the California mission system had collapsed, leaving behind graveyards filled with the remains of thousands of Indians.

In Sonoma, the mission courtyard and surrounding grounds serve as a final, unmarked resting-place for untold numbers of natives who lost their freedom, identity, and their lives through a cultural upheaval that was most certainly beyond their comprehension.

The adobe mission built by Sonoma's Indians is open to the public as a museum. Its cool, dark hallways, quiet sanctuary, and many rooms filled with shadows of the past offer a sense of spiritual or ghostly activity. The most common experience is an abrupt, isolated change in temperature that can be experienced throughout the mission and its courtyard. In addition, there are occasional sightings of a hooded person in gray robes who appears in the shadows of the sanctuary. This apparition may be Father Altimira returning to look after his church.

Mission Solano also served as a place of refuge and a burial site for local settlers who developed fatal illnesses. The spirits of these pioneers may be looking for someone to take them back to their homes now that they are free of their mortal bodies.

GEORGE YOUNT GRAVE SITE

Yountville Cemetery
Jackson Street and Lincoln Street
Yountville, CA 94599
(707) 944-0904 (Chamber of Commerce/Visitor Center)

George Calvert Yount was the first white man to settle in the Napa Valley. He arrived in 1831 after an arduous journey from Kentucky. When he surveyed the lush valley and noted its potential for agriculture, he said, "In such a place I should love to clear the land and make my home. In such a place I should love to live and die."

Yount carried out his wishes. With the help of local Indians and a Spanish land grant, he built a blockhouse and mill on his Caymus Rancho and established himself as master of the Napa Valley. In 1865, he founded the town, Yountville, that bears his name and he built a fine mansion that still stands within view of the motorists on Highway 29. George lived a long and prosperous life in the valley. Engravings on Yount's massive tombstone list such accomplishments as "first U.S. citizen to be ceded a Spanish land grant; skilled hunter, frontiersman, craftsman, and farmer; he was the true embodiment of all the finest qualities of an advancing civilization, blending with the existing primitive culture; friend to all." George Yount died on October 5, 1865, at the age of seventy.

George Yount's life was not all success and happy days. On May 2, 1852, his only son, Robert, and his wife, Pamela S. Grigsby, died. Both were in their mid-twenties. Their grave is only a few feet from that of George and his wife, Eliza.

There are many reports of an elderly gentleman resembling George Yount making appearances near the old mansion on Washington Street and at the Yount gravesite. He appears as a partial apparition, fading in and out. He seems to hover near the grave of Robert and Pamela, creating cold spots. The tragic loss of his son and daughter-in-law in a county still considered a frontier must have weighed heavy on old George.

Based on several reports, the early evening is the best time to experience ghost activity in the Yountville cemetery. In addition to George Yount, other spirits roam this large graveyard, which contains not only pioneers but also the remains of hundreds of Indians in unmarked graves. These native Californians venture out to see what we have done with their beautiful Napa Valley.

MARE ISLAND CEMETERY

Mare Island Naval Reservation
Contact: Navy Yard Association of Mare Island
PO Box 2034
Vallejo, CA 94592
(707) 562-1812

On June 13, 1892, fifteen sailors from the USS *Boston* were sent ashore on Mare Island Naval yard to prepare ammunition. A short time after they entered the magazine, a huge explosion killed them. It is thought that one of the men dropped a shell and the concussion lead to the disaster. A beautiful marble memorial, erected by their shipmates, stands as the focal point of the Mare Island Naval Cemetery. It lists the names of those fifteen sailors, marking their final resting spot. The tragedy of their deaths was recently publicized with the news that this cemetery, under the former jurisdiction of the Bureau of Yards and Docks, may no longer be maintained by the Navy after closure of the shipyard. These men and many others may be abandoned, leaving their graves to be watched over only by the spirits of those resting below the stately monuments.

Mare Island Naval Cemetery was founded by the famous American war hero, Commodore David G. Farragut, who arrived there in September of 1854. Soon after the grounds were marked, the place began to fill up. In 1863, eight Russian sailors lost their lives fighting a fire in San Francisco. They were buried at Mare Island, thousands of miles from home.

Anna Arnold Key Turner is buried near the USS *Boston* monument.

She was the daughter of Francis Scott Key, author of the *Star Spangled Banner.* Anna lies next to her daughter, Anna Turner.

Nine hundred graves fill the 2.4-acre cemetery. Some of them are marked only with a name while others give a fascinating history of the deceased.

The ghosts of this historical cemetery tend to appear at dusk or dawn. Many visitors have seen thin, pale apparitions of amorphous shapes marching or slow stepping across the grounds. Some of the graves have rather large cold spots, suggesting that more than one person resides in the grave. Ghost hunters have reported the sounds of rattling chains, maybe anchor chains, and canon fire, marching troops, orders shouted by officers, and whispers, most often by feminine voices.

OLD BODEGA SCHOOLHOUSE

Bodega Road
Bodega, CA 94922
Sonoma County
(707) 875-3422 (Bodega Bay Area Chamber of Commerce)

Known as the setting for one of Alfred Hitchcock's best films, *The Birds,* the Bodega Schoolhouse is now a private residence and a documented haunted place. Built in 1873, the large two-story building served as schoolhouse and social center for this rural community seventy miles north of San Francisco. Generations of Bodega residents were educated there. Many of them enjoyed adult social activities in the second-floor rooms, such as plays and dances, until the building was closed to the public in 1962. In 1974, the current residents moved in, restored the place, and converted it to a private residence. Since then, many observations of ghost activity have been made, some of them documented by investigators from the television program, *Sightings.*

Ghostly activity inside the building includes sounds of children playing, a woman singing, bumps on the walls, steps on the stairs and in the hallways, voices in the hallways, door knobs turning, a rocking chair that rocks without the touch of any visible being, and sounds of a large, noisy party in the second-floor room that served as a community social hall. The *Sightings* investigators also observed, and filmed, a light fixture swinging over the stairway.

Outside the building, people have observed apparitions and the sounds of children playing. On one occasion, tourists stood at the gate waiting for a little girl to move off the steps so they could photograph the entry to the historic building. The little girl descended the steps, moved toward the tourists, and disappeared as her foot touched the ground. Others have seen an apparition of variable intensity and duration along the sides of the building in areas that might have been a favorite play area. More often, the sounds of children at play can be heard without trespassing on the property.

JACK LONDON STATE HISTORICAL PARK

2400 Jack London Ranch Road
Glen Ellen, CA 95442
(707) 938-5216.

Jack London (1876-1916) was at one time the most famous and most highly-paid writer in the world. He grew up in Oakland, educated himself after failing to find worthy teachers at the University of California, and embarked on a fantastic career as a gold miner, war correspondent, short story writer, novelist, playwright, farmer, rancher, sailor, and socialist.

After the turn of the century, Jack became disenchanted with city life in Oakland and San Francisco. Turning to nearby Sonoma County, he discovered a paradise in the Valley of the Moon and settled on twelve hundred acres near the small town of Glen Ellen. It was there that he wrote many of his greatest novels and stories while developing a keen interest in agriculture. He built a ranch as an experiment, employed many workers, including ex-convicts, supported as many as four hundred people at one time, and entertained some of the world's greatest thinkers at his swimming pond and dinner table. About eight hundred acres of Jack's ranch is open to hikers and tourists. The ranch house in which he died, the ruins of his massive Wolf House that burned in 1913, and his gravesite are accessible to the public.

Jack London suffered from declining health throughout the final ten years of his life. Most of the time, he was able to ignore his illness and be happy, living on the ranch with his devoted wife, Charmian. It was Charmian who made the first sighting of Jack following his death on November 22, 1916. In her memoir, she wrote that some months after his death, she had a vision of him, "As clearly as ever I had looked upon the man, I saw Jack stepping blithely in the green domain [field in front of the ranch house] . . . whistling comradely to an unmistakable friend shadowing his heel—Peggy the Beloved, our small canine Irish saint." It is believed that this observation was made from the front porch of the ranch house.

Over the decades, many psychically sensitive people have attempted to contact Jack London or experience the ether of his spirit at various locations on the ranch. The strongest contacts were at the stone ruins of the Wolf House. It was here in 1913 that Jack watched his greatest dream go up in a huge blaze and, of all the places on the ranch, it is this site that would most likely tie Jack to our physical world. Charmian once wrote that on the fateful night of the fire "something in his heart burned out that night and was lost forever."

Clearly, his spirit was transformed by the fire, the kind of event that would lead to an earthly bond between the deceased Jack London and his Wolf House. Indeed, thin apparitions have been seen in the huge foyer and great hall of the massive ruins. Whether these apparitions were Jack, one of the many workmen who built the place, or even Charmian London, no one can say with certainty.

The best time to roam the ruins in search of ghostly activity is near sunset in the winter months, late November in particular, near the anniversary of Jack's death.

Another place for worthwhile investigation is the ranch house. The room in which he died and his den are open to visitors. Good places to learn about Jack London and obtain historical information, photographs, and maps, are Charmian London's House of Happy Walls on the Jack London ranch, now open as a museum, and the World of Jack London Bookstore in Glen Ellen.

ANGEL ISLAND

Hospital Cove, officer's quarters, graveyard, Angel Island State Park

Ferry boat Service: Vallejo (707) 643-3779; Alameda (510) 769-5500; San Francisco (415) 929-1543

This beautiful island, with the prophetic name, is indeed haunted but it was not named for those good spirits that inhabit the many ruins of its Civil War-era military facilities. Spanish explorer Juan Manuel de Ayala entered San Francisco Bay on August 5, 1775, and anchored his tiny ship, the *San Carlos,* in a sheltered cover of an island he named Isla de Los Angeles (Island of the Angeles). Nearly two hundred years later, the inhabitants of Angel Island experienced strange happenings created by the ghosts of this haunted island.

Throughout the Civil War years, and the later years of the nineteenth century, many military installations were erected on the island to house troops and their families, prisoners of war, and quarantined immigrants. Many of these buildings stand vacant and open to exploration by ghost hunters.

At Camp Reynolds, a long row of officers' houses still stands around the parade ground. The house closest to the Bay was the home of the commanding general and his family. The ghost of an elderly lady dressed in dark clothing is often seen on the porch of this house. She sits in a rocking chair staring at the parade grounds that slope downward to the bay. She is seen in daylight hours but she fades away when approached by ghost hunters.

Other ghosts appear at many of the civilian and military ruins scattered around the island. The first murder on Angel Island occurred in 1854, when two men argued over a boat. Eddie Fiefirst started quite a dispute when he attempted to dismantle a boat, owned by Captain Payne and himself, in Hospital Cove. Both dashed away from the beach to get their guns and, apparently, each fired shots. Fiefirst was the better shot, however, and succeeded in killing Captain Payne. The captain's ghost still roams the beach at Hospital Cove, keeping watch over the boats moored there.

In 1858, two friends, U.S. Commissioner George Pen Johnston and State Senator William I. Ferguson, dueled at Quarry Point. In front of one thousand witnesses, these men traded several shots before each was wounded. Johnston survived, but his wounded opponent Ferguson suffered for days with an infection before dying. Legends surrounding the duel suggest that Johnston begged Ferguson for forgiveness but the dying man refused to speak to him. Now, a brooding ghost wanders the plateau above Quarry Point, harboring resentment and anger toward his former friend.

Perhaps the most tragic event in Angel Island's history occurred May 23, 1872. Emma Spohrs, fifteen years old and the belle of the island, attended an evening of dinner and dancing in honor of Company H, scheduled to depart the island within days. She was escorted by her father, Patrick Spohrs, but followed about by an ardent admirer, Sgt. Fritz Kimmel. According to witnesses, Kimmel was peculiarly silent during the evening, possibly due to a rebuke received from Emma earlier in the day. Whatever transpired between them, Kimmel was moved to madness. About midnight, he walked up to Emma's left side, placed a gun at her temple and pulled the trigger. Within moments, he turned the gun on himself and fired. Official reports attributed this tragedy to Kimmel's infatuation with the young lady who, it seemed, had no interest in him.

Emma was buried at Camp Reynolds on May 26, 1872 in grave forty-five. Kimmel was buried the next day in grave forty-six.

The hall at Camp Reynolds, where this tragedy occurred, stands in ruins on a bluff overlooking the main camp. It is a brick building, obviously of Civil War vintage. The place is not open to visitors, but sensitive ghost hunters exploring the exterior of the site have experienced strange auditory phenomena believed to be the fateful party of May 23, 1872.

Angel Island is currently a state park, accessible by ferry boat from San Francisco, Vallejo, and Sausalito. The best way to explore the island's numerous ruins and scenic points is by bicycle. The eight-mile perimeter road is easy for most occasional cyclists.

A small bookstore at Hospital Cove offers maps, guidebooks, and brief histories to direct ghost hunters to sites for visiting the tragic days of Angel Island.

MISSION SAN RAFAEL

1104 Fifth Avenue
San Rafael, CA 94901-2502
(415) 456-3016

In 1817, Father Luis Gil established the Mission San Rafael on the shores of San Francisco Bay. The sunny region, with dryer air and less fog than other Bay Area mission locations, provided a healthier environment for American Indians weakened by the white man's diseases. Soon after it opened, the mission became known as an asistencia or sanitarium. Many American Indians who went there from other missions were restored to good health by the merciful care of Father Gil. Others were too far gone and died soon after arriving in sunny San Rafael. They are buried in unmarked graves on the mission grounds.

By 1821, the mission was a thriving community under the new leadership of Father Amoros. Over one thousand American Indians lived there in 1828 and the place became a base of operations for military exploration of northern and eastern California. In 1829, the mission was attacked by natives who resisted the church's intrusion into their lands. Three years later, twenty-one pagan Indians were killed by church neophytes led by Father Mercado. Peace returned to the mission as the California missions were secularized. In 1837, General Vallejo became administrator of the mission structures and lands.

Mission San Rafael was torn down by Americans in 1861 but Saint Rafael's church was built on the site in 1869. This structure burned in 1919. A replica of the original mission was constructed in 1949. The edifice is probably not on the original footprint of the old mission.

A hooded figure, no doubt Father Gil, is often seen walking through the walls of the newer structure as he passes down what might have been an aisle or hallway of the original mission. Also, candle flames sometimes emerge from the walls of the mission replica. One ghost hunter reported the muted moans of sick and dying Indians as he walked the grounds of St. Rafael's church. It is likely that these sounds were heard as he walked over the unmarked graves of American Indians who sought good health at Mission San Rafael.

CAVENAUGH INN

10 Keller Street
Petaluma, CA 94952
(707) 765-4657

This beautiful Victorian-era inn was the home of Adelaide

Adelaide Cavenaugh raised seven children in this house. She died elsewhere but she returned to look after guests at this charming Petaluma inn.

Cavenaugh in the late nineteenth century. This industrious woman raised several children in the house over a period of about twenty years. Legend suggests that she died elsewhere while longing to return to her Petaluma home.

Soon after the inn opened for business, footsteps were heard in the Magnolia Room. Locked closets would open and shut with no apparent help. This ghost also enjoys human contact. She often brushes the cheeks of male visitors, assuming this ghost is Adelaide. The ghost of Cavenaugh Inn is playful and polite, and likes to keep the place neat and tidy. Coins left in a pile late at night are often found in neat stacks in the morning.

CHINA CAMP

China Point Regional Park on San Francisco Bay
Exit Highway 101 onto North San Pedro Road
San Rafael, CA 94901-2520
(415) 456-0766

During the latter third of the nineteenth century, a large Chinese community developed on the north shore of San Francisco Bay. At first, the community was composed of a small group of renegade fisherman. Their dwellings were so crude that the place became known as China Camp. After the turn of the century, China Camp was a small town with a few stores, drinking establishments, and wooden shacks that housed about five hundred people. In the early days, the Chinese fishermen operated outside the law, using drift nets to catch shrimp and other fish. Their activities served as the basis of several short stories by Jack London. In his *Tales of the Fish Patrol,* and the short-stories, "Yellow Handkerchief" and "Yellow and White," London describes his exploits against the fisherman of China Camp as a member of the fish patrol (forerunner of the state fish and game wardens). Yellow Handkerchief, so named because of a yellow bandanna tied about his head, was the outlaw of a band that caught illegal shrimp and the raided oyster beds of San Francisco Bay.

Encounters with law enforcement officers often resulted in violence. Some shrimpers were shot or drowned. Other tragedies that befell this community included fires that almost destroyed the camp and the great earthquake of 1906.

Some of the residents of old China Camp, who lost their lives over a century ago, still occupy the place. While sitting on the quiet beach, visitors have heard Chinese spoken in muffled tones. There are several cold spots, probably at sites where shacks once stood before going up in flames. One of the best sightings at China Camp was a vision of a Chinese fishing boat that appeared a short distance offshore. The boat was about thirty feet long. Six to eight men were seen on deck as the boat glided into the shallows with its sail slack. Upon touching the beach, the boat disappeared.

GREENWOOD MANSION

Northwest corner of Airport Road and Highway 29 (entrance to Napa Valley Airport) between Napa and the town of American Canyon, 94558.

On the evening of February 9, 1891, Captain John Quentin Greenwood worked in his yard mending a fence. Two well-dressed men, William Roe and Carl Schmidt, approached on foot asking for food. Something about their demeanor troubled the captain, so he refused their request and ordered them off his property. Enraged, the two men attacked Greenwood and forced him into the kitchen where they poured a sedative down his throat, then administered chloroform. When Greenwood's wife, Lucinda, returned from visiting a neighbor, she found the men in her kitchen. She attempted to flee but the thieves dragged her into the bedroom, tied her hands and feet, and drugged her. Roe and Schmidt then searched the house for valuables. Before leaving, Roe strangled Lucinda Greenwood as she lay on the bed.

After drinking for an hour or two in nearby Napa, Roe and Schmidt returned to the Greenwood house. They found John Greenwood at his wife's feet, completely distraught over her death. Roe dragged him into the hallway on the second floor and shot him twice in the head. Although Lucinda had been dead for at least two hours, he shot her in the head as well.

Schmidt was apprehended in Denver in May of 1892, convicted of armed robbery and sentenced to life in San Quentin. Roe was not caught until late 1896. He was hanged in front of the old Napa Courthouse on January 15, 1897. This was the last public execution in California.

John Greenwood miraculously recovered from his wounds. His emotional wounds, however, did not heal. He never again entered the second-floor bedroom where Lucinda died. In constant mourning for his wife, he moved her wagon into a room and slept in it until he died several years later.

Today, the Greenwood mansion is used for administration offices for the Napa Airport business park. Several cold spots have been

In 1891, Lucinda Greenwood was murdered in this Napa house. Years later, her grief-stricken husband, John, died here, anxious to join his wife in the spirit world.

detected in parts of the house in what were the kitchen and the second floor hallway. One sensitive visitor reported of hearing a soft moaning on the second floor. Another ghost hunter reported a faint apparition of a woman floating down the hallway. Lucinda's murder and the years of misery that befell John Greenwood are intriguing to ghost hunters.

BARTHOLOMEW PARK WINERY

1000 Vineyard Lane
Sonoma, CA 95476-4845
(707) 935-9511

This winery opened its doors in 1993, but the building it occupies is over a century old. At times it served as a woman's prison, a hospital, and a morgue. During those times, lives were lost under horrifying circumstances and some of the deceased continue to make the old

Batholomew Park Winery in Sonoma was a prison for women and a morgue. Spirits roam its cellar.

building their home. A short time after the winery opened, employees heard voices singing in the cellar that once housed prisoners. The choir is heard in the afternoon and again late at night. Hymns are the usual choice. These ghosts do not like modern music, especially the stuff that comes out of boom boxes. Once, a tape player was pushed off a table by a ghost. Occasionally, modern tape players are tolerated if older styles of music are played. *Greensleeves* is a favorite with the ghosts of Bartholomew Park Winery.

Bartholomew Park Winery is open for tasting. Adjacent to the picturesque winery is a little park available to visitors for picnics.

VALLEY OF THE MOON SALOON

17154 Sonoma Highway (Hwy 12)
Sonoma, CA 95476-3326
(707) 996-4003

This popular Sonoma Valley saloon occupies a two-story building that is over 120 years old. It is home to a ghost that has not been identified. This ghost seems to like things kept in proper order. If employees leave drawers or pantry doors open, they are soon closed by an unseen entity. Chairs and other furniture are often moved and lights are turned off. Records in the jukebox are sometimes moved onto the turntable. In the upstairs apartment, a tenant once watched a bar of soap float in the air as if the ghost suggested he needed bathing. In 1993, a fire swept through the second floor. No cause has been found. Today, the apartment is restored and the saloon is a favorite for local ghost hunters. Many believe the building sits over an ancient American Indian burial ground.

LACHYMA MONTIS

General Vallejo's Home
300 W. Spain Street
Sonoma, CA 94576-5623
(707) 938-1519 (State Historical Park Headquarters)

Under the Mexican government, General Mariano Vallejo was the

General Vallejo died at his Sonoma home in 1890—Lachyma Montis—after a long career as military commander of northern California and central figure in the Bear Flag revolt of 1846.

military commander and director of colonization for northern California under the Mexican government, from 1834 to the annexation of the region by the U.S. in 1846. His vast holdings included 175,000 acres of land that, together with his nearly limitless military and civil powers, made him the most powerful man north of Monterey. General Vallejo made his home in Sonoma, initially in a large adobe named La Casa Grande that still stands on the plaza as a reminder of the Mexican period of California history. In 1846, the general was rudely awakened and dragged from La Casa Grande by members of the Bear Flag Revolt.

Following annexation of California, the general continued to be influential in California's governmental, social, and economic affairs even as his vast empire slipped from his grasp. In 1850, he purchased about twenty acres of land a half-mile from Sonoma's plaza at the foot of a mountain where a spring flowed. Local Indians called the place "crying mountain." General Vallejo translated the name to Latin,

Lachyma Montis, and so named his estate. On this land he built a Victorian mansion and several out buildings that supported vineyards, orchards, gardens, and yards of livestock. In spite of the apparent prosperity of the little paradise, Vallejo's fortune declined to a point of financial distress, forcing him to live his final years in austerity. He died at Lachyma Montis in 1890 at the age of eighty-two, having witness the transformation of California from a wilderness to a sophisticated economic power.

Vallejo's house, gardens, and brick barn are open to the public. The 140-year-old Victorian mansion is restored and offers many quiet places for ghost hunters to experience the presence of Vallejo or members of his large family. One local ghost hunter saw the apparition of a small woman, dressed in a flowing white gown, descend the narrow staircase.

CAPTAIN ALFRED EASKOOT

3548 Shoreline Highway
Stinson Beach, CA 94970.

In 1984 the little town of Stinson Beach gained notoriety from something other than sharks attacks. Locals and tourists began seeing a hazy figure roaming the foggy beach, dressed in a maritime officer's uniform. According to a UPI story, dated October 30, 1984, the figure is the ghost of Captain Alfred Easkoot, who died in 1905. Apparently, while serving as a cabin boy on board a sailing ship, Alfred lost his hand in a fire. The lost appendage was replaced by a hook that served the captain well throughout his maritime career. Upon his death, Alfred was placed in a coffin and his remains were carried across the beach as part of the burial process. At one point, the pallbearers lost their grip and the coffin was dropped, spilling the dead captain onto the sand. In their haste to put the corpse back into the coffin, the hook was dislodged and lost in the sand. Now the captain's ghost wanders Stinson Beach in search of his hook.

Sightings are most likely under foggy conditions, late in the afternoon or early evening. One report states that Captain Easkoot is seen nearly every night at 2 A.M. as he leaves the old wooden house and heads for the beach. The captain conducts his search at the north end of the beach. He is sometimes seen at Duxbury Reef, northwest of the beach, the site of at least three shipwrecks.

The house, built of wood from the captain's old ship, is now a private residence. It has been resold several times over the past twenty years due to intolerable ghostly activity.

COMMANDANT'S HOUSE

Old Benicia Arsenal
Benicia, CA 94510-3210
Benicia Historical Society: (707) 745-1822
Commandant's Residence: (707) 747-9458

In 1860, General Julian McAllister assumed command of the U.S. Army Arsenal at Benicia. Many believe that he remains at his post today. Officially, his command ended in 1866, but after so many years, including the dramatic Civil War years, he seems to have found it impossible to give up his mansion on the grounds of the historic arsenal.

Among the many buildings General McAllister built during his tenure is the commanding officer's house, Arsenal building No. 28, but it is not typical of most of the military structures of the Civil War years. Built in 1860, in a style described as Greek Revival, the beautiful white mansion stands two stories tall with Doric columns decorating the balustrades that enclose the wide verandas. Over the years, the interior has been remodeled several times to accommodate various military administrative operations.

In the 1980s, the mansion was converted to a restaurant. Several workers and patrons experienced ghosts during this time. A male figure has been reported, appearing as a hazy, transparent entity. He is quiet, but his appearances are accompanied by cold spots. There are no published reports of detailed sightings, but persons associated with the historical preservation of the Arsenal may offer more information to serious investigators.

The commanding officer's mansion was investigated by well-known ghost hunter and parapsychologist, Lloyd Auerbach. He was unable to verify the nature or extent of the haunting. People familiar with the mansion and its history believe that the general is back and in command. The commanding officer's mansion is undergoing restoration as a museum.

BEAR FLAG REVOLT 1846

Sonoma Valley Visitor's Bureau
453 First Street East
Sonoma, CA 95476
(707) 996-1090

In the 1840s, Sonoma was a gathering place for adventurers and settlers who had crossed the Great Plains and Rocky Mountains of America. They came for land, business opportunities, climate, and freedom from the confinement of Eastern society. They also came because Mexico held a rather loose rein on the northern California territory. As their numbers increased, they gained influence in the area. Talk of annexation grew louder and attracted more supporters. On June 14, 1846, acting with the knowledge that an American fleet was en route to Monterey, forty Americans captured the little presidio on Sonoma's plaza, imprisoned the region's military governor, General Vallejo, and raised a makeshift flag, the Bear Flag. These revolutionaries proclaimed the California Republic a free and sovereign state, with allegiance to the U.S., and maintained a grip on the Sonoma region for nearly a month. When Commodore Sloat arrived in Monterey and raised the U.S. flag in July of 1948, the "Bear Flaggers" graciously capitulated stood by as the Stars and Stripes were raised on their flagpole.

The drama and historical importance of this event is commemorated by the Bear Flag monument that sits on the northeast corner of Sonoma's town plaza. On quiet summer evenings, or dark wintry nights, a heaviness sometimes gathers in the air around the monument with a quiet rumbling, perhaps indicating the presence of the Bear Flaggers or some remnant of the great emotion they shared during their brief revolution. Had their revolution failed, all of them would have been executed. Some sense of vibrations or reverberation from the event may be experienced by lying on the ground near the monument and meditating on the bold action of the men who gathered about the flagpole on that June day in 1846. This type of haunting activity has been experienced throughout the years on battlefields and other places of military action.

GHOSTS OF FIRST STREET, BENICIA

Historical District
First Street
Benicia, CA 94510-3210
(707) 745-2120 (Chamber of Commerce)

Benicia is an old town, founded in 1846 by Robert Semple, with the assistance of General Vallejo. The expectation was that the riverside town would become the commercial hub of northern California. Named for Vallejo's wife, Benicia, the town was promoted and developed in a hurry by its first citizens, but it was overshadowed by San Francisco. By 1850, it became clear that the economic, social, and political goals of its founders would not be realized.

Benicia did achieve some political success, though, by serving as California's state capital from 1851 to 1856. Furthermore, establishment of the army's arsenal at the eastern border of Benicia in 1849

Benicia's historic district includes this building that served as the State Capitol from 1851 to 1856.

The Frisbie-Walsh House, built in 1851, is one of many old homes in Benicia's historic district.

has led to more than a century of military presence in the town and construction of some of the areas most interesting historic buildings.

The main thoroughfare through old Benicia is First Street. It slopes downward from the city park at Military Highway to the waterfront. Along both sides of the streets, and on many side streets, are century-old buildings still used as shops, restaurants, and bars. A walking tour of old Benicia takes the tourist past the oldest and best documented structures such as Jurgeson's Saloon at the foot of First Street to the Union Hotel, the State Capital Building, Stumm's Store, and the Congregational Church. On side streets, many Victorian-era homes still stand. Among the most historic are the Frisbie-Walsh House (c. 1850) at 235 East L Street, the Riddell-Fish House (c. 1890) on K Street between Second and Third Streets, the Carr House (c. 1870) at 165 East D Street, and the Salt Box House at 145 West D Street.

Some residents from Benicia's historic days still roam the streets of this charming town. One kindly old man, who looks to be about sixty years of age, appears in work clothes and stands at the entrance to alleyways with his dog. The man greets passersby in a clear voice and appears quite real as his dog sits at his side. A moment later, the man and dog are gone. Patrons at some of the bars on First Street are familiar with this man but no one knows his name, when he died, or his reason for haunting this spot.

Visitors to shops on First Street often tell of cold spots in these old buildings and a frequent sense that someone is standing behind you, looking over your shoulder. Still others report creaking floorboards, swinging doors, and peculiar odors, such as cigar smoke, that signal the return of a ghost from Benicia's past. By all accounts, the ghosts of First Street display a welcoming, benevolent attitude toward modern visitors who pass through their beloved old town.

CHAPTER 3

San Francisco Peninsula

By separating the Bay from the Pacific Ocean, the San Francisco Peninsula extends northward from the Silicon Valley to the magical city-by-the-bay, San Francisco. A wide variety of ghost-hunting sites can be found in the quaint, small towns of the peninsula, the deserted beaches and rocky promontories washed by the Pacific Ocean, and the City of San Francisco. More than two hundred years of history have left numerous Victorian mansions, bars and restaurants, schools and colleges, ships, bridges, libraries, and graveyards that offer great opportunities for ghost hunting.

MOSS BEACH DISTILLERY

Overlooks the ocean at the corner of Ocean and Beach Streets
Moss Beach, CA 94038
(650) 728-5595

This popular oceanside restaurant and bar has been featured on the television shows *Judge for Yourself, Unsolved Mysteries, In Search of . . .,* and *Sightings.* The building was constructed in the 1920s as a home. Sometime in the late 1920s or early 1930s it was converted to a bar in which illegal liquor was sold and other nefarious activities were conducted. Legend tells of a woman who died on the beach below the restaurant. She was involved with some of the characters who frequented the bar. She might have be murdered on the beach or, in the heat of an argument, pushed from the cliffs. In any event, she is attached to the Moss Beach site. Her ghost, dressed in a blue dress, has been seen in almost every room of the restaurant, including the foyer outside the lady's room.

There may be other ghosts at the Moss Beach Distillery. Strange happenings such as bar stools flipping over, lights going on and off, and silverware disappearing from the tables have been observed by employees and partrons. The cliffs adjacent to the restaurant, and the small beach below, are particularly eerie. For many years, regular dinner-hour presentations with psychics entertained patrons with channeling and ghost stories. Call the restaurant for information about current events.

THE PRESIDIO OF SAN FRANCISCO

On the shores of San Francisco Bay, bordered by California Street on the south, Lincoln Boulevard on the west, and Highway 101 to the east
www.sfvisitor.org

In 1769, a band of explorers was sent north from Southern California by General Juan Gaspar de Portola. Their orders were to search for a bay that local Indians claimed lay several days' march from the settlement of Santa Barbara. On November 1, 1769, Jose Francisco Ortega and his scouts discovered San Francisco Bay. They wandered along the western shore until they came to a bluff overlooking the entrance to the bay. We now call that place the Golden Gate. Upon the arrival of the main body of explorers and troops, General Portola established a military facility at this place to protect the bay from intrusion by other imperial nations. It was christened Punta del Cantil Blanco, or White Cliff Point. By 1794, the Spanish had constructed adobe walls and small buildings, and placed several bronze cannons in the fort. The harsh climate soon destroyed the little fort. The adobe walls melted in the rain and the bronze and iron cannons became useless. By 1812, Mexico gained independence from Spain and the San Francisco Bay region became Mexican territory. The new military commanders recognized the need for a larger facility that enabled short-range cannon fire control of the Golden Gate. A Presidio was established on the shores of the bay that also encompassed some of the high ground near the old Punta del Cantil Blanco.

Over the 185 years of its existence, the Presido has grown to include nearly three thousand acres where a variety of military establishments have come and gone. Among the lasting landmarks are several Civil War era houses and buildings and a large military cemetery. Nearly all of the occupants of this cemetery lost their lives on foreign ground, or on ships at sea, but their spirits have come home to San Francisco. Several sightings have occurred here, ranging from life-like figures in military uniforms, some of whom speak to visitors, to wispy apparitions that flash by in an instant. Several cold spots have been reported in this graveyard as well.

Some old brick houses and officers' dormitories are haunted, but these are not open to the public. A number of houses on MacArthur Avenue make up Officers' Row. Most of these homes were constructed before the Civil War. They continued to serve as officers' quarters until the Presidio was closed as a military facility in 1994. Over the decades, hundreds of career officers and their families enjoyed the comfortable houses, surrounded by well-kept grounds and the exciting city of San Francisco. This duty station was a favorite and offered much more than the dusty outposts of Kansas, Texas, and other army facilities in the U.S. and overseas.

Some of the dearly departed who lived there were so attached to the Presidio of San Francisco that, after their deaths, they returned to Officers' Row. The sidewalk and porches of these old homes are favorite haunts of spirits. Wispy images of women in Victorian gowns and men in uniform are often seen strolling the neighborhood or sitting on the verandas and porches on Officers' Row.

The Presidio Performing Arts Theatre opened as the base movie house in 1939. In the World War II years, it was the site of shows for service men and women. Many big bands played there. Comedian Bob Hope entertained troops there prior to their departure for the war in the Pacific. The place has a very strong 1940s atmosphere.

Near Crissy Field, percipients have reported a strong sensation of being pulled downward into the ground as they walk about, viewing the old buildings. It has been described as a heaviness of the limbs, then a feeling of profound muscular fatigue. The gait becomes slower as energy seems to leave the body. The feeling may be counteracted by taking one's mind off the old buildings and historical events of the Presidio.

One visitor described this phenomenon as a time warp, as though one were being pulled into another time in the history of the Presidio.

MAMMY PLEASANT'S GHOST

Corner of Octavia and Bush Streets
San Francisco, CA 94109

Mary Ellen, known as Mammy Pleasant, arrived in San Francisco from New Orleans in the early 1850s. Her mother was a free black woman. Her father was a Cherokee Indian. She had one blue eye and very high cheekbones that gave her a distinct appearance among the local black population. She practiced a kind of voodoo magic and blackmail. She used both as a means of gaining control over several wealthy people in the city, including Thomas Bell, an investment banker. She established herself in his mansion as the housekeeper, overseeing several servants and exerting considerable control over Bell's personal life. She coerced him into marrying one of her black-mail victims who had become Bell's mistress. That relationship proved to be a wild one. Bell's wife tried to run away with jewels and other valuables but she was arrested. Mammy Pleasant interceded with the police and managed to have the woman returned to the household without civil punishment.

Legend tells of Bell and Mammy Pleasant amassing a fortune by practicing voodoo among some of the city's wealthy people. They worked well together until October 16, 1892, when Bell fell from a third floor balcony after a fierce argument. Mammy's red scarf was found with his body but no charges were brought against the eighty-six-year-old woman. Mammy continued to dominate the Widow Bell's household until 1896, when she forced her out of the mansion without money or any of the other fruits of her nefarious business. She took up residence in a grove of trees near the mansion. From this sanctuary, the demented woman attempted to work her voodoo magic, without success, on people who walked by the place. She died penniless and homeless at the age of ninety-two.

For decades after her death, the Bell mansion was known as a haunted house. It burned in the 1920s, but Mammy's ghost continued residing in the trees. Many people in San Francisco swear that she is there to this day. She emerges from hiding among the trees, trying to work her old magic on unsuspecting passersby. A hospital now occupies the former site of Mammy Pleasant's home, once known as the "Bell House of Mystery."

ALPINE INN

3915 Alpine Road
Menlo Park, CA 94028
(650) 854-4004

This rustic bar was opened in 1853 as a stagecoach rest stop offering a change of horses and over-night accommodations to weary travelers. Today, the Alpine Inn is a popular weekend destination for mountain bikers, motorcyclists, and others arriving from the nearby Silicon Valley and Stanford University communities. Generally, the affluent clientele comes seeking a calming experience in the wooded Portola Valley. The Alpine Inn offered the best burgers in the area and very cold beer.

Adjacent to the bar is an outdoor area for barbecues and alfresco drinking. It is here that the wispy image of a bearded gentleman is sometimes seen. He appears to be dressed as a horse wrangler with heavy boots, a cowboy hat, and a bandana tied around his neck. There is no specific information about the history of the Alpine Inn that might identify this ghost. He may have been an employee of the stagecoach line, having met his death while handling horses that were kept here. In the rough and tumble days of the 1850s and 1860s, he might even have been the victim of a barroom fight, or an outlaw awaiting the departure of the stagecoach.

SAN FRANCISCO COLUMBARIUM

1 Loraine Court
San Francisco, CA 94118-4216
(415) 752-7891

Built in 1898, this stately structure is a blend of Roman, Baroque, and English architectural designs. Its stained-glass windows and quiet ambience create a perfect resting place for the remains of more than eight thousand people. Some of them were prominent figures in the city's tumultuous past, including members of famous families such the Stanfords, Folgers, and Magnins. Among its ordinary residents are the remains of a little girl named Viola Von Staden. Viola, and the Columbarium, survived the earthquake of 1906. In the days and months that followed, the city burned and the people suffered in many ways. Clean drinking water, unspoiled food, and adequate shelter were in short supply and unavailable in many parts of the city. Little Viola drank water from polluted wells and became ill. She died at the age of seven in 1907 in her bedroom in a house that once stood near the Columbarium. Her ashes are kept in a brass urn in a niche also occupied by the ashes of Anna Von Staden (1867-1958) and Christina Von Staden (date unknown).

Little Viola seems to like the Columbarium, for her apparition has spoken to caretaker, Emmitt Watson. One afternoon in 1997, while Emmitt stood on a ladder, he heard a little girl speaking. Thinking that a visitor was heading his way, he descended the ladder. A little girl stood in front of the Von Staden niche. As he walked toward her, she disappeared. At the time, Emmitt did not recognize her as Viola Von Staden. Later, when he mentioned the episode to her descendents, they produced a photograph of Viola. Emmitt recognized the child in the photograph as the very same one he had seen in the Columbarium in 1997.

Other niches in the Columbarium contain the remains of some of the city's quirky citizens whose sense of humor dictated rather bizarre burial arrangements. Barbara Fernando's ashes lie in two 150-year-old tobacco canisters. Antique martini shakers adorn the niche of Norman White while the ashes of the man below him sit beside a bottle of Johnny Walker Red and a shot glass.

ALCATRAZ ISLAND FEDERAL PRISON

Golden Gate National Recreation Area, Fisherman's Wharf, San Francisco

San Francisco Visitor's Bureau: (415) 391-2000; www.sfvisitor.org

Boat Schedules: Red and White Fleet Pier 41 (415) 546-2700 or 929-1543; Blue and Gold Fleet (415) 705-5555

This very strange place has been investigated by several psychics and organizations that evaluate paranormal events. Psychic Sylvia Brown was asked by the Park Service to determine what was causing the screams and crying often heard in the dungeon area of Cell Block C. Sylvia made contact with a former occupant named Butcher who resisted her efforts to help his soul find peace. Prison records indicate that a hit man named Abie Maldowitz, nicknamed Butcher, was killed by other prisoners in this area.

Cell Block D has several cells where visitors have heard voices. Cell 14 has an icy cold area in one corner. People who contact this cold spot often feel unsettling emotions. Records show that Cell 14 housed a murderer named Rufe McCain, who was in solitary confinement for three years.

Cells 11, 12, and 13 may also be visited. These cells elicit strong emotional reactions from most people, who often experience a spiritual presence. There are stories of banjo music in the shower room. It seems this place was favored by Al Capone for music practice.

Long before Alcatraz became a federal prison in 1922, local Indians considered the place inhabited by evil spirits. The island is crawling with spirits of American Indians, prisoners, and others who lost their lives there, so ghost hunters may experience haunting activity anywhere on the island. Visitation is allowed only with a tour group accompanied by park rangers. Night tours of the prison are offered for those who feel they can withstand the scary atmosphere. Proper preparation and an ability to mentally block out the modern world can help the visitor hear the screams and cries of the dead on Alcatraz Island.

FLORA SOMMERTON: GHOST BRIDE OF CALIFORNIA STREET

On California Street, between Powell and Jones Streets
San Francisco, CA 94108

In 1876, the parents of Flora Sommerton arranged a marriage with a gentleman who was much older than their teenage daughter. Flora hardly knew the man, but their marriage would have provided her family with many advantages, including a higher social status. On the eve of the wedding, while trying on the white gown, Flora realized she had only one course open to her. She dashed out of the house, ran up California Street, and disappeared. Fearing some crime had taken place, perhaps a kidnapping, the family offered a large reward.

A claim for the reward was not made until 1926, when Flora was found dead in a boarding house, some sources call it a bordello, in Butte, Montana. She was dressed in the same wedding gown she wore when she made her escape from San Francisco in 1876. Her body was brought home and buried in the family plot.

Perhaps Flora still feels trapped, for she runs up California Street, sometimes in the middle of street, but most often on the sidewalk. Anyone standing in her way is cast an angry glare. One ghost hunter felt a cold spot pass over him while another reported pressure as though Flora's hand pushed him aside.

GOLDEN GATE BRIDGE

San Francisco Visitor Information Center:
(415) 391-2000
www.sfvisitor.or

In 1771, Juan Gaspar de Portola sailed the California coast in search of a legendary bay. One morning, he was at the right place at the right time. The tide carried his leaky ship eastward, toward shore, just as the fog lifted. Ahead, he spotted an opening in the rugged coastline, about 1.25 miles wide. That break in the coastline was the only entrance to the fabled bay. Other explorers had failed to find it since Vizcaino's first exploration of the coast in 1603.

Soon after the Americans took California from the Mexicans in 1846, travel across the mouth of San Francisco Bay became frequent as city residents established businesses in what is now Marin, Sonoma, and Mendocino counties.

In the early part of the twentieth century, ferryboats carried large numbers of passengers between Sausalito, Tiburon, San Rafael, and San Francisco. Sometime in the late 1920s, the idea that a bridge could span the gap was introduced.

The project began in 1932 with construction of two huge towers that stood about 1.1 miles apart. The engineering is so perfect that the towers are actually five inches wider apart at the top than at the base to account for the curvature of the earth. During construction of the foundations for these towers, at least three workers fell into the flowing wet cement, buried alive and forever entombed in the base of the Golden Gate Bridge.

Soon after the bridge opened, it became a popular place for committing suicide. Since 1936, over six hundred people have hopped the railing and thrown themselves to death. The drop from mid-span to the water's surface is 286 feet. From that height, the velocity upon impact is so great that the effect on a human body is the same as hitting concrete. It is believed that the actual number of suicides is much greater.

Jumpers seem to prefer the east side of the bridge. This affords a beautiful view of San Francisco and the East Bay cities as they fall to their death. A few murders have occurred on the bridge as well.

A walk along the east rail after dark, especially when the fog rolls in, is the best time to experience the manifestations of several spirits who haunt the Golden Gate Bridge. Some people have reported screams that trail off into the distance, cold spots, and places in which a foreboding sense of misery and sadness occurs. A few lucky ghost hunters have seen apparitions perched on the east rail, facing the icy water below. One apparition turned to the ghost hunter and cried, "Help me!" just before she jumped.

CRISSY FIELD AT THE PRESIDIO

On the shores of the bay
Marina Drive
San Francisco, CA 94108

About 1910, the U.S. Army established an aviator training center on the shores of San Francisco Bay. The broad field adjacent to the beach seemed perfect since prevailing winds were quite constant through the Golden Gate. The ground was leveled and a grass field was planted. From 1913 through 1922, the Ninth and Ninety-first Aero Squadrons were based at the site, trained in air combat, then sent overseas.

Crissy Field at the San Francisco Presidio was used for pilot training during WWI. The grass runway is now a recreation area.

Many of them lost their lives in France during World War I. Several other pilots lost their lives during training. Student pilots, and others who were simply unlucky, got caught in shifting winds off the bay and suffered fatal accidents on or near Crissy Field. In 1938, the field was paved, but flying was curtailed due to obstructions imposed by the Golden Gate Bridge. In 1968, the army discontinued fixed-wing aircraft flights at Crissy Field. Helicopters used the field until 1977.

Today, Crissy Field is hardly recognized as a landing strip. Portions of the old asphalt runway have become part of a parking lot for fisherman, wind-surfers, and joggers who frequent the area. Old runway markings can still be found under wind-blown sand. A few historical markers briefly describe the importance of the site during World War I.

When the wind stops blowing, and there are few people around, ghost hunters have heard the clatter and roar of old biplanes. Others, when walking the length of the old runway, felt an ominous sensation of being pulled downward into the ground. Another odd experience often reported there was a sudden shift in the wind. The nearly-constant westerly breeze can make a sharp swing around and come from the east, then make an abrupt return to a westerly orientation. People familiar with the operation of small aircraft will recognize this as the propeller blast from airplanes as they taxi into position for take-off.

CLIFF HOUSE

1090 Point Lobos Avenue
San Francisco, CA 94121-1449
(415) 386-3330

The Cliff House sits at the very tip of San Francisco on a rocky perch overlooking the Pacific Ocean. Sometimes the sun sparkles on the blue waters spreading to the horizon. More often, fog shrouds the rocky Point Lobos and raging waters thrash the rocks below. This creates an atmosphere of danger and intrigue. Several people have drowned in these waters. At least ten fishermen over the past twenty years have been washed from the rocks by the surf. Between 1870 and 1900, at least five boats ran aground there with loss of life.

The Cliff House at Point Lobos was constructed in 1863 as a rest stop and dining establishment for travelers coming up the coast from Pacifica and Half Moon Bay. The city of San Francisco was, at that time, several miles east across the sand dunes and wooded hills of the peninsula. Travelers coming from the city used the Cliff House for entertainment. Rumor suggests several of its rooms were used as a bordello.

Among the travelers to visit the Cliff House were three U.S. presidents and the wealthy businessmen of San Francisco.

In 1881, San Francisco mayor Adolph Sutro bought the Cliff House and added an elaborate swimming facility supplied with freezing cold water from the ocean. The huge restaurant and inn burned down on Christmas Eve, 1894. Sutro replaced it with an eight-story French chateau that burned in 1907. In 1909 Sutro's daughter, Emma, built the structure that exists today.

The best place to experience the aged atmosphere of the Cliff House is outside, on the walkway between the building and the cliffs. When the fog is thick, it is easy to travel in our mind back to the Victorian era. Several ghosts of people who lost their lives on the treacherous rocks of Point Lobos have been seen floating over the walkway.

FORT POINT—SENTRY AT THE GOLDEN GATE

Golden Gate National Recreation Area
Long Avenue at Drive, under South Tower Golden Gate Bridge
San Francisco, CA 94121-1449
(415) 556-1693
www.sfvisitor.org

Standing in the shadow of the Golden Gate Bridge, this lonely remnant of a very distant historical period possesses an intense ghostly atmosphere. Cold, dark, brick corridors, bastions, and casemates still fitted with massive cannons offer quick passage to another time, putting the sensitive visitor in touch with spirits who still stand guard on the ramparts or practice gunnery.

The first fort on this site was a crude adobe and log facility constructed by Spanish soldiers in 1794. By 1821, the tiny fort fell into

Fort Point was completed in 1861, just in time to protect San Francisco Bay during the Civil War. This haunted fort stands under the Golden Gate Bridge.

disrepair from neglect and the harsh San Francisco climate. This decaying outpost served little purpose until 1846, when it became a military objective of the Bear Flag revolt. Kit Carson led a group of Americans across the Golden Gate and up the sandy slope to attack the poorly-manned fort. Later, the strategic importance of the site was recognized by the U.S. Army.

Construction of the present fort was begun in 1854 and completed in 1861. Together with gun emplacements on Alcatraz, and at Fort Lime Point near the present town of Sausalito, Fort Point was America's primary means of defending San Francisco and Northern California from foreign encroachment.

Despite its extensive armament, Fort Point never fired a gun in battle. Instead, the lonely fort slipped into disrepair and decay by the turn of the century. Fortuitous circumstances saved the fort from destruction when the Golden Gate Bridge was constructed in the 1930s. After extensive renovation, the essence of an era has been revived.

As visitors to Fort Point pass down the dark, deserted corridors, the sounds of soldiers living on the very frontier of America, far from home, mix with the roar of surf surging against the outer walls. Many soldiers came to this desolate place with a sense of apprehension over the harshness of life and duty at the fort, and a longing to return to civilized America. Some lost their dreams amid the tumultuous history of the opening of the West to never return to the East or Midwest. A few of these lost soldiers still stand guard at Fort Point on the Golden Gate.

BANK OF AMERICA BUILDING

555 California Street
San Francisco, CA 94104-1501
(415) 622-3456

This very tall, unique commercial building was constructed in the late 1960s on land that was once at the very edge of San Francisco Bay. Poltergeist activity started there in the early 1970s with papers and books flying off desks, and telephones rising into the air. Cold spots have been noted on several floors as well. No reports of apparitions have been made, but some ghost hunters surmise that apparitions would be there. The spot on which the building rests was part of the Barbary Coast, a vast collection of bars, houses of prostitution, and gambling establishments that were popular during the wild days of early San Francisco.

Poltergeist activity may be from the earthquake of 1906, too, since it seems to increase when small earthquakes or strong winds cause a shudder to pass through the building.

MANSIONS HOTEL

2220 Sacramento Street
San Francisco, CA 94115-2327
(415) 929-9444

This popular hotel has been thoroughly investigated and found to be haunted by a number of spirits. The establishment is comprised of two mansions joined to make a hotel. In the oldest part of the hotel, visitors may see documents on display that attests to the hauntings. These documents include affidavits of witnesses, photographs of ghosts, transcripts of seances, and other interesting information. The place has been studied by the Office of Paranormal Investigations of JFK University and the noted psychic, Sylvia Brown. Many guests have experienced cold spots, unexplained noises, and objects flying about. Some visitors have seen a female apparition. During a séance in 1991, several people saw the same apparition. Scientific investigations have revealed strong electromagnetic forces in the old part of the hotel. The newer of the two mansions is not haunted.

SAN FRANCISCO ART INSTITUTE

800 Chestnut Street
San Francisco, CA 94133-2206
(415) 771-7020

Sometime in the 1870s, the old cemetery on Russian Hill became overgrown with the rapidly expanding city. After the rubble of the

Part of the San Francisco Art Institute was constructed in 1906 over a cemetery. Ghostly footsteps are heard in its tower.

1906 earthquake was cleared away, a building that resembles a monastery was constructed adjacent to the cemetery. Headstones were pushed aside by other construction, leaving the souls of the dearly departed without access to their graves. It seems they found a way to their resting sites via the building that now houses the San Francisco Art Institute.

The place has been recognized as a haunted site for at least fifty years. Footsteps are sometimes heard in the tower. They often proceed to a doorway, then some invisible force opens the door. During remodeling of a portion of the building, an evil presence was perceived by several people. Psychics were called in to contact the ghost(s). The psychics determined that several frustrated ghosts were in the building. Perhaps their passage to the old cemetery was obstructed by the remodeling of the place.

WHITTIER MANSION

2090 Jackson Street
San Francisco, CA 94109-2840
(415) 567-1848

This mansion, built in 1896, originally served as the home of William F. Whittier until his death in 1917 at the age of eighty-five. The twenty-one years he spent in the house must have been sufficient to entice continued residence to this day.

In the basement, a cold-presence is often noted, as is a shadow on the walls. Could this be Mr. Whittier? The other possibility is that the ghost may have something to do with World War II. From 1938 until 1941, the house served as the German consulate. During those pre-war years, German spies worked out of the mansion gathering information on naval facilities and ships in San Francisco Bay and other military installations. At times, the cold presence is experienced in other parts of the house, but it seems to be most often noted in the basement where most of the clandestine activities were no doubt carried out.

CARMELITA COLEMAN

The Peninsula School
920 Peninsula Way
Menlo Park, CA 94025-2358
(650) 325-1584

This beautiful, Victorian-style mansion was built in 1880 as a wedding gift from John Coleman to his wife, Carmelita. While preparing to move into the house, Carmelita was accidentally shot by a pistol John kept. He was so distraught by this tragic event that he refused to enter the house. However, Carmelita did take up residence there after her death. She has appeared as a green apparition to several credible witnesses. Carmelita's home became a school but she is not upset by the heavy traffic of students and teachers. On one occasion, she appeared before twenty students and a teacher. Her ghost remained for more than five minutes. She roams the hallways enjoying the mansion built for her.

Newly-married Carmelita Coleman died from a gunshot wound only a few days after moving into the Menlo Park mansion her husband built as a wedding gift.

FERRY BOAT, EUREKA

Hyde Street Pier Maritime Park
San Francisco, CA 94109
Maritime Park of San Francisco
(415) 556-3002
www.sfvisitor.org

This massive ferryboat, launched in 1890 and kept in service until February 10, 1957, carried passengers daily from San Francisco to Oakland. Before the opening of the Bay Bridge, the *Eureka,* and her sister ships were the only means of traveling between the East Bay and the City. In the hours after the 1906 earthquake, the *Eureka* carried thousands of frightened citizens away from the devastated city and the San Francisco peninsula. Records show that the *Eureka* never had an accident that resulted in loss of life, but a number of police reports were filed for missing persons who were believed to have traveled on this boat.

Suspicions are high that a number of people committed suicide by jumping from her decks into the icy waters of the bay. There may have been a murder or two on board as well.

Percipients have seen the wispy figure of a woman who desperately races from one end of the ship to the other. Others have seen the apparition of an old man sitting on one of the long wooden benches, gazing out the window. Several cold spots have been discovered near the side railings and at each end of the ship.

THE TALL SHIP, *BALCLUTHA*

Hyde Street Pier Maritime Park
Fisherman's Wharf, San Francisco
Maritime Museum of San Francisco 94109
(415) 556-3002
www.sfvisitor.org

The tall ship, Balclutha, *rounded treacherous Cape Horn several times in the 1880s, collecting the spirits of sailors lost at sea.*

This beautiful, square-rigged, tall ship was built in Glascow, Scotland, and launched in 1886. She is over 300 feet in length with three masks rising 145 feet above the deck. She served many years, hauling coal from England to San Francisco. On the return voyage to England, she carried grain from the San Joaquin Valley loaded at San Francisco wharves. These 10,000-mile voyages took her through tropical heat, freezing cold, and many storms. She rounded treacherous Cape Horn several times.

As with many sailing vessels of her day, men died on board. Health care was non-existent. Several sailors died of chronic illnesses such as diabetes and lung disease while others succumbed to hard labor.

Most of those sailors were buried at sea, but several decided to remain on board. The *Balclutha* is a spooky ship, especially below decks when no one is around. Odd sounds are heard, including the muted sounds of moaning sailors struggling through their final minutes of life. Sometimes visitors feel the cold presence of someone standing behind them or cold spots near the crew's quarters. A cold spot is often detected near the foremast on the starboard side of the ship. This may be the spot where a sailor landed after falling from the tall mast during a gale off Cape Horn.

DALY CITY BART STATION

500 John Daly Boulevard
Daly City, CA 94014-3849
(415) 989-2278

The Bay Area Rapid Transit (BART) system opened in the 1960s. Its high-speed, subway-like trains connect the distant parts of the sprawling Bay Area, making it possible to get from Concord or Fremont to Daly City in less than one hour. The trains have an excellent safety record, but the stations can be dangerous late at night when few people are around.

Some of the stations in the system have been the site of murder and other heinous crimes. Some people have lost their lives on the trains, dying from heart attacks or strokes. For some unknown reason, many spirits of people who died on a BART train, in a BART station, or near a station, have chosen to ride to the end of the line. They get off at Daly City and wait on the platform for a train that will take them to some other destination within the system. The partial apparition of a woman carrying a brief case has been seen in the early morning hours. She stands facing the tracks but disappears when trains arrive in the station. One percipient reported a well-dressed older man who asked, "When does the next train to Berkeley arrive?" Upon turning to face the gentleman, he faded away.

HOOVER TOWER, STANFORD UNIVERSITY

1 Stanford University El Camino Real at University Avenue
Palo Alto, CA 94306-1123
(650) 723-2300

Stanford is known as a challenging and demanding institution of higher learning. As with all institutions of its caliber, there is an occasional student who is overwhelmed by the work, disappointed with his progress, or pushed over the brink into a well of depression. In the decades since Stanford opened it doors, at least a few students have lost their lives in or around the Stanford campus.

The apparition of a young man is often seen as he walks past the Hoover Tower on the path that lies on the north side, heading in an eastward direction. He appears to be in a hurry as he carries his books. One person observed him in the early evening. He glared at her and said, "I'm late!" Then, the image disappeared. The young man appeared to be dressed in clothing from the 1920s or 1930s and his hair was dark, shiny, and combed back away from his face. This fellow may have died near the Hoover Tower.

CHAPTER 4

South Bay Area

Until the late 1970s, the South Bay Area was composed of small towns and ubiquitous orchards and vineyards. The peaceful country environment was dotted with old farmhouses and other buildings that captured the lingering essence of long-past historical eras. The explosive growth of the Silicon Valley industries wiped out almost all the open space as cities surrounded or paved over historic buildings and built new structures on historic sites. As the pace of modern development accelerated, many towns recognized the value of the local historic legacy. Hundreds of charming buildings from the nineteenth century have been preserved and many back roads to fascinating places take the visitor away from the modern rush of the South Bay Area and its Silicon Valley.

TOYS "R" US

130 East El Camino Real
Sunnyvale, CA 94087
(408) 432-0331

From the outside, Toys "R" Us in Sunnyvale appears to be too busy, too well-lighted, and too modern to be haunted, but it is the home of a stubborn ghost who refuses to move onward to the Light. Inside, the store is a whirlwind of activity, yet employees and shoppers have reported ghostly activity. Stuffed animals fly from the shelves, wall mountings move, a variety of sounds are heard including footsteps and wood chopping, faucets in the restrooms run then stop, and cold

This modern toy store is haunted by John Johnson, who died on this land in 1884. Psychic Sylvia Brown spoke to this ghost and captured his image on film.

spots are all part of the daily activity. Employees arrive for work in the morning only to find merchandise piled on the floors or restacked in peculiar shapes. Ghostly activity has been experienced at almost any time throughout the day and night, suggesting that this ghost is always vigilant or protective of something.

Psychic research has revealed that the Toys "R" Us ghost is John Johnson, also known as Yonny (Yonny is the Swedish pronunciation of the nickname Johnny). Yonny was a gold rush forty-niner who settled in the Santa Clara region in the 1870s. He became a minister of a small local church and roomed with a farming family that occupied the land on which Toys "R" Us rests. Sylvia Brown discovered that Yonny was in love with the daughter of a wealthy, prominent judge and businessman. Since his poor circumstances made his wish for marriage impossible, he spent his days longing for the beautiful Beth while he labored on the farm and preached in his church.

Beth married another man in 1881, which some think sent Yonny into a state of depression. In 1884, while chopping wood, the story goes, his thoughts wandered to his unrequited love and he injured himself. Yonny bled to death somewhere on the land occupied by this modern toy store.

Yonny has been seen by Sylvia Brown and his image has been captured on film. Communications with him have clarified his reasons for haunting this Sunnyvale site. He is waiting for his love, the beautiful Beth, to pass by and notice him. Even when informed that he and Beth are dead, he insists that he must stay on the farm and await her interest. Beyond that, Yonny feels a need to "look after things." He is perplexed by the modern store and ways of modern people and believes he must do something to prevent the future from intruding on his time period in the 1880s.

Yonny has manifested his presence throughout the large store, but among the best places to experience him is on the shelves of stuffed animals, especially the Teddy-bear section where he rearranges the toys, and the restrooms where he turns water on and off.

WINCHESTER MYSTERY HOUSE

525 South Winchester Boulevard
San Jose, CA 95128-2537
(408) 247-2101

Sarah Winchester's massive, sprawling mansion in San Jose is a must for every Bay Area ghost hunter. Known as the "house built by ghosts for ghosts," its bizarre architectural features, dark hallways, cold spots, and thick air are a clear sign that ghosts live there in a world quite different from ours. The 160-room Winchester Mystery House has stairways that disappear into the ceiling, doors that open from the upper floors into mid-air, and wandering corridors that caused many of the workmen who constructed the place to become lost. The house is dominated by the number thirteen: there are thirteen bathrooms, thirteen steps on many staircases, ceilings with thirteen panels, chandeliers with thirteen lights, and many rooms with thirteen windows. But throughout the mansion there are only two mirrors, because mirrors were believed to frighten ghosts away and

Many ghost hunters believe the Winchester Mystery House in San Jose is one of the most haunted buildings in America. Ghosts instructed Sarah Winchester to build 750 rooms.

Sarah Winchester had no wish to be inhospitable toward her friends from the spirit world.

In 1883, at the age of forty-four, Sarah Winchester was widowed and inherited the Winchester Rifle fortune, which amounted to twenty million dollars, plus an income of one thousand dollars per day. This fortune did not diminish Sarah's depression over the deaths of her husband and baby daughter, Annie. While seeking solace from a psychic in Boston, Sarah was told that spirits demanded that she move to the West Coast, build a beautiful home of the most costly materials, and that construction must never stop, day or night. When she inquired about the last directive, Sarah was told that as long as construction continued, she would remain alive. The psychic added that this construction project, funded by profits from the sale of Winchester rifles, would be restitution to those many spirits who lost their lives to Winchester firearms during the Civil War and Indian Wars.

Frightened, yet dedicated to the psychic directives, Sarah moved to

San Jose, purchased a small farmhouse that stood on 161 acres of land, and began building her monument to the spirit world. Construction continued nonstop for thirty-nine years as Sarah followed daily instructions from spirits who spoke to her in her seance room. Despite her obedience, she died on September 5, 1922. At the moment of her death, workmen walked off the job, leaving rooms unfinished and nails partially driven.

Today, only 160 of the estimated 750 rooms remain. A labyrinth of hallways, secret passageways, dead-end staircases and many odd-shaped rooms with low ceilings await visitors who tour Sarah's house. The seance room, and Sarah's bedroom containing her deathbed, are the two most fascinating chambers. In these rooms, sensitive visitors have reported hearing chains rattling, whispers, footsteps, cold spots, icy breezes, and even apparitions. Professional psychics and ghost hunters such as Sylvia Brown have reported these phenomena, plus organ music and strange lights that flow across walls or flash out of nowhere. Sylvia Brown also reported seeing the ghosts of a man and woman, caretakers of the Winchester estate at the turn of the century, who are unhappy about the many visitors to the house. They watch over Sarah Winchester's home with great devotion.

Many investigators believe other ghosts inhabit the house, including American Indians, soldiers, bandits, and cowboys from all over the Old West. After all, the place was designed by ghosts as a home for ghosts on earth.

A guided tour is the only way to gain entry to the Winchester Mystery House. Great adventures in this haunted house take place on the Friday the Thirteenth candle-light tour and the Halloween tour. Either way, this place is one of the best houses in the Bay Area, accessible to the public, with a documented presence of ghosts.

BELLA SARATOGA

14503 Big Basin Way
Saratoga, CA 95070-6011
(408) 741-5115

This charming, Victorian-style house was built in 1895 by Samuel

Soon after moving into this house, Sam Cloud ran into the street where he was hit by a streetcar. He died in the front room on the second floor. A few years later, his wife died in the same room.

H. Cloud. Not long after moving in, Sam walked into the street in front of the house to look around the neighborhood. Being unfamiliar with the sounds of traffic on the street, he failed to recognize the meaning of a clanging bell and the shouts of people standing nearby. Sam was injured by a derailed streetcar as it careened down the sloping street at high speed. He was taken into the house where he died in the front room on the second floor. The house remained in Sam Cloud's family until the death of his wife many years later. Soon after the new occupants moved in, odd things began to happen.

Since then, employees and patrons of businesses in the old Cloud house have experienced many strange things that can only be the haunting activities of ghosts. Many people have felt something swish by them without the possibility of an opened door or window. When least expected, doors and windows open by themselves, lights go on and off, and objects are moved or hidden. Several employees have seen the figure of a young woman dressed in white. This ghost has been seen climbing the stairs to the second floor as well as next to the bar on the main floor. This woman may be Sam Cloud's wife, or one of his children, who remains to look after Sam. His ghost may be among those who cause so many odd noises and strange happenings at the Bella Saratoga.

MISSION SAN JOSE

43300 Mission Boulevard
Fremont, CA 94539-5829
(408) 657-1797

This large mission was founded June 11, 1797, at a site fifteen miles north of the city of San Jose, to avoid interaction between Spanish soldiers stationed in the South Bay and local Indians converted by the priests to mission life and the Catholic faith. At one time,

Mission San Jose, located in Fremont, was the site of an Indian revolt in 1828. Spanish soldiers and Indians are buried here.

Mission San Jose had more Indians than any other northern California mission. In accepting the mission lifestyle, dictated by the Franciscan priests, the Indians were exposed to measles and smallpox brought by Spanish soldiers who visited the mission in 1805. Within eighteen months, one-third of the mission Indians were dead. Many of them were buried in unmarked graves in the cemetery adjacent to the north wall of the church.

Despite this tragedy, the Indian population grew to almost two thousand by 1825. This population explosion created friction between the priests, who had established themselves as absolute rulers over the native Americans led by tribal elder Estanislao. In 1828, Estanislao gathered his loyal followers and turned against the priests in armed conflict. Several soldiers, who rushed to the mission from the town of San Jose, were killed along with many of the Indians. Estanislao survived the conflict and, with the intervention of Father Duran, escaped punishment. He lived at the mission another ten years before he died.

Today, Mission San Jose has several sites for ghost hunting. The patio and church cemetery are good places to search for spirits. Many Indians worked at mission trades in the patio and lived in quiet desperation while longing for their old, beloved lifestyle. Most ended up in an unmarked grave in the shadow of the tall adobe church that they built. The cloister, a long building fronting the street, has a broad porch that offers many shady spots for lingering spirits to watch the modern world roll by.

Sightings have been reported at the unique half-circular steps at the front of the church. These steps, built by Indian labor, were covered with the soil of passing decades and forgotten until they were revealed during a restoration in the 1970s. On these steps, late in the afternoon, cold spots have been experienced with occasional areas of "heavy" air, suggesting the presence of ghosts sitting upon the steps. It is possible that some of the Indians who built the steps, and all the mission buildings, have claimed this place as their own, having paid with their lives and their culture.

Or perhaps the Spanish soldiers killed by Estanislao and his warriors sit upon these steps clinging to the church they defended in 1828.

OPERA HOUSE

140 Main Street
Los Gatos, CA 95030-6814
(408) 354-1218

The only performances that take place at the Los Gatos Opera House are weddings and other ceremonies. The 1904 vintage building was once a music hall, hosting at least a few operas along with several concerts, plays, and other social events. The impressive building has been used for a variety of businesses and renovated several times. The last renovation occurred after the 1989 Loma Prieta earthquake that nearly destroyed the place.

A variety of odd things have occurred in the building over the years. One, documented on photographic film, occurred in 1992. Photographer George Sakkestad snapped twenty-five shots of an employee in various locations throughout the building. When the

This 1904 Los Gatos music hall hosts weddings, concerts, plays, and a ghost caught on film.

film was developed, two frames revealed a shadowy figure standing on a balcony. The dark figure could not be the result of a film processing accident because a clear image of the white balcony is seen in front of the figure. There is no information about this ghost. It could be the restless spirit of an actor or singer waiting to go on stage, or to receive the attention of visitors to the Opera House.

RENGSTORFF HOUSE

3070 North Shoreline Boulevard
Mountain View, CA 94043-1341
(650) 961-5321 or 903-6088

The classic, two-story Victorian mansion was built in 1867 by a German immigrant, Henry Rengstorff. Henry arrived from Germany, via Cape Horn, in 1850. He worked his way up from farm laborer, to farmer, then major landowner and developer of the area,

The magnificent Rengstorff House was built in 1867 for a large family. Many died here but their spirits could not leave their beautiful home on the shores of San Francisco Bay.

later known as Mountain View. After amassing a small fortune, he built a 4,000-square-foot, twelve-room mansion in 1867. He married Christine Hassler, also a German immigrant, and together they raised seven children: Mary, John, Elise, Helena, Christine, Henry, and Charles. When Rengstorff died in 1907 at the age of seventy-seven, his daughter, Elise Rengstorff Haag, moved in with her husband and Perry, the orphaned son of Elise's sister, Helen. Perry inherited the house, then sold it in 1959 to a development company. The place sat empty and fell into disrepair. It was scheduled for demolition in 1980. The local community saved the house, moved it, restored it, and opened it to the public in 1991, when it gained a reputation as being haunted.

Little information exists about events that may have occurred there. Henry and his daughter Elise died in the house and no doubt other family members died there, too. Those who entered the place after 1991 reported the sound of crying and odd bumps against the walls. Some visitors reported seeing the image of a young woman, possibly Elise or Rengstorff's wife, Christine, standing at the front windows on the second floor.

The Rengstorff House is now available to rent for receptions and parties. Tours are conducted on Sunday, Tuesday, and Wednesday from 11 A.M. to 5 P.M., as an example of Victorian architecture and the local lifestyle of the 1860s in Mountain View.

ROSICRUCIAN EGYPTIAN MUSEUM

Corner of Mabley Street and Park Avenue
San Jose, CA 95126
(408) 947-3600

One experienced world-traveler remarked that the Rosicrucian Egyptian Museum in San Jose has more artifacts than some of the museums in Egypt. This is not an exaggeration, for the Rosicrucian contains thousands of items, ranging from bits of jewelry and perfume bottles to tools and mummies from the oldest dynasties of ancient Egypt. The museum even contains a replica of a tomb, enabling the visitor to experience the ambience of wall drawings, sacred rooms carved from solid rock, and an empty crypt left as though grave robbers had been there only minutes before. The whole place has an aura of heavy air as though the weight of three thousand years of history and countless lost spirits settled there.

While gazing into the empty eye sockets of an Egyptian priest, it is hard to imagine that his spirit is not close by, guarding his remains that were removed from his sacred resting-place ten thousand miles away. Other mummies in the museum, and cherished items taken from graves and other sacred places, must also be guarded by ancient Egyptian spirits. Indeed, the heavy atmosphere, ancient artifacts, human remains, and the aura of the mysterious Egyptian religion produce an atmosphere perfect for ghost hunters. They can practice meditation techniques for removing one's self from the present world to another place and time at the Rosicrucian Egyptian Museum.

BLOOD ALLEY—HIGHWAY 17

From The Cats Restaurant to Scott's Valley

Highway 17 winds its way from the Santa Clara Valley, through the coastal mountains, to the beach at Santa Cruz. Along the way can be seen majestic views of wooded valleys, redwood groves, fog-filled canyons, and pastures dotted with horses. The twenty-two-mile passage is a beautiful drive, but also one of the most dangerous in America. Highway 17 is known as "Blood Alley" by local law enforcement agencies.

Since 1980, twenty-seven people have lost their lives in traffic accidents on Highway 17. Sharp curves, sudden changes from clear air and good visibility to dense fog, and an undivided four-lane roadbed contributed to the tragedies. Another factor is careless driving by people speeding to or from the Santa Cruz beach and boardwalk. Many head-on collisions occur as tired or intoxicated drivers cross the double line into oncoming traffic. Even though no crosses or other monuments mark the places where so many have died, the dangerous segments of the road are apparent to first-time travelers on Highway 17. Sharp curves and other hazardous segments are good places to hunt for ghosts. Turnouts allow for parking and roaming about the roadside.

Some drivers have experienced auditory phenomena such as the sound of screeching tires or the crashing together of automobiles. Others have had seen white, transparent, amorphous clouds standing on the roadbed. One motorist reported an icy presence in the passenger seat of his car as he drove around horse-shoe bend, a long, sharp turn which has been the site of many accidents.

The north end of Blood Alley is marked by the Cats Restaurant, a well-known local watering hole and eatery of great character. The southern end is at the bottom of a steep grade where Highway 17 enters Scott's Valley. Anywhere along this route is fertile ground for ghost hunting.

VILLAGE LANE

Sushi Yokohama (formerly Lisa's Tea Treasures)
336 N Santa Cruz Avenue
Los Gatos, CA 95030-6814
(408) 395-1990

Perfect Nails (formerly Kids Trading Company)
348 N. Santa Cruz Avenue
Los Gatos, CA 95030-6814
(408) 395-5259

In 1868, the little village of Los Gatos, nestled against the eastern slope of the Santa Cruz Mountains, faced a problem. An old woman had died of pneumonia after her cabin filled with a surge of cold water from a flash flood. At the time, Los Gatos had no official cemetery. A local farmer, John Mason, donated a small tract of land at the east end of town to house the community's dearly departed. The graveyard filled as farming accidents, shootings, and hangings took the lives of the careless, the unlucky, and the criminal residents of Los Gatos. In addition, fatal, infectious diseases took the lives of the very young and very old, adding to the number of residents in the oak-tree-shaded graveyard. By 1890, the cemetery was running out of space and its borders could not be expanded. The town had grown rapidly, crowding the graveyard on all four sides.

Many of the shops of charming Village Lane in Los Gatos were built over a graveyard. And the ghosts don't like it.

The town council decided to move the cemetery to another site. Many relatives were contacted and asked to move the remains of their loved ones. Most people complied. However, some family members could not be found while others refused to move the graves of their loved ones. So, the gravestones of the remaining graves were turned face down and construction of new roads and building proceeded.

In the 1950s, a crew digging a new sewer line along Village Lane uncovered a small, cast-iron coffin containing the remains of a child. They also uncovered gravestones. Until this time, local residents and shop-owners had not realized that they occupied buildings over the final resting-place of many dead people.

Reports were made of strange noises, radios found blaring when a shop-owner arrived for work in the morning, and other strange happenings. At Lisa's Tea Treasures, now Sushi Yokohama, a doorbell rings at odd times when no one passes through the door. Several other shops, bordered by North Santa Cruz Avenue, Village Lane, and

Highway Nine, have been the sites of haunting activity. Sometimes ghosts are actually seen, like the dark-haired woman who wanders through several shops. Perhaps she is the wife of John Mason, whose son, Paul, refused to move his mother's grave in 1890.

Evidence that the ghost of a little boy, Willie, has been gathered by local ghost hunters. Willie died of pneumonia at the age of two, one day after coming home from a San Francisco hospital. He had been hospitalized for a long time in order to have his clubfeet corrected by surgery. In 1958, at the corner of Highway 9 and North Santa Cruz Avenue, workmen uncovered little Willie's gravestone. He was buried in 1889, according to his sister, Nellie Turner Denning, who recorded pertinent information in 1958. She described Willie as a beautiful boy with "golden ringlets all over this head." He was playful and always seemed happy. Perhaps his ghost is the one that haunts the Kid's Trading Company, a children's clothing and toy store on Village Lane.

DOUBLE D'S SPORTS BAR

254 N. Santa Cruz Avenue
Los Gatos, CA 95030-6814
(408) 395-6882

This popular eating and drinking establishment is one of many businesses located over the old Los Gatos Cemetery Several graves were left there in 1890 as the town grew. The entire block is the site of several ghostly happenings. One of the curious things about the site occupied by Double D's Sports Bar is that all of the previous businesses located here failed in less than five years. Many were well-run, popular restaurants, but success eluded the owners, perhaps because the restless spirits whose bodies were buried beneath didn't like anyone occupying their space.

Visitors to the sports bar have experienced the usual cold spots, the rush of wind, and the feeling that someone was looking over their shoulder. The latter happens most often in the men's room. Some people speculate that the ghost of little Willie frequents the sports bar since it sits almost on top of his grave.

This popular bar sits over a graveyard. Several previous enterprises in this building failed after a brief run, possibly due to restless spirits.

LE BARON HOTEL

Wyndham Hotel and Resort
1350 North First Street
San Jose, CA 95112-4709
(408) 453-6200

In the early 1980s a tired, lonely salesman checked into room 538 at the Le Baron Hotel after many days on the road. It seems the man was unable to escape the stress and fatigue of his life, so, after checking in, he checked out. The cause of his death was a drug overdose according a *UPI* story (February 5, 1982). In 1984, a magazine, *San Francisco Focus,* announced that the man was still occupying room 538. His ghost has been seen by housekeeping staff and guests. The most frequent manifestations are cold spots and a sense of sadness. At times, the ghost is seen swishing down the hallway or hanging out near the front desk.

BROOKDALE LODGE

Eleven miles northwest of Santa Cruz on Highway 9
P.O. Box 9
Brookdale, CA 95007
(408) 338-6433

This charming, rustic resort was built in 1923 in a manner that blends the structure with the stately redwoods and fern grottoes of the Santa Cruz Mountains. It sits between the quaint villages of Ben Lomond and Boulder Creek, not far from the bustling Silicon Valley. In the 1940s, Brookdale Lodge was a getaway destination for many celebrities including Rita Hayworth, Joan Crawford, Marilyn Monroe, Bob Hope, and President Herbert Hoover. Throughout the fifties and sixties, it attracted visitors from all over the U.S. Among its unique features is a stream that runs through the lodge, fostering the growth of ferns and mosses. Redwoods also grow within the lodge and blend with the rustic décor.

Brookdale Lodge is a pleasant, relaxing place but spirits do roam in the old resort. Big band music is sometimes heard echoing through the bar area. Glasses move or break without any identifiable cause. Voices sometimes call out to others and a cold rush of wind may be felt in several locations as ghosts sweep by visitors.

The playful ghost, Sarah, a young girl who drowned in the stream that passes through the center of the lodge, is often seen near television sets and radios. An older lady, believed to be Sarah's mother, is sometimes seen in the main lobby, called the Brook Room.

The ghost of a boy believed to be twelve years old has been observed in room forty-six. A lumberjack named George and a woman named Mary have also been identified among the spirits that haunt Brookdale Lodge. A number of psychics have investigated this place and have found at least forty entities there.

MISSION SANTA CLARA

500 El Camino Real
Santa Clara, CA 95050-4345
(408) 554-4023

In 1776, Russian activities in northern California made the Spanish nervous. Spain believed that a reasonable, non-military deterrent would be the establishment of more missions in the San Francisco Bay area. Thus, supplies and resources that had been ear-marked for a mission in southern California were sent north to the area that is now the city of Santa Clara. On January 12, 1777, the Mission Santa Clara de Asis was established on a broad, fertile plain populated by several Indian villages.

A disastrous flood destroyed the mission on January 23, 1779, but a cornerstone for a new church was laid November 19, 1781. The new building was one of the most elaborate in the mission system and, for many years, it enjoyed great prosperity. Today, the Mission Santa Clara sits on the grounds of Santa Clara University and functions as a Catholic church.

In 1814, Father Jose Viader enjoyed a reputation as being something of an athlete. His muscular physique and stamina was widely admired and helped him convert the local Indians to the Catholic faith. Marcelo, a large Indian who had resisted efforts of the mission fathers to convert native inhabitants, attacked Father Viader one night. Even with the help of two other Indians, Marcelo could not overcome the strength and speed of Father Viader. The Indians were defeated but Viader forgave them. From that point on, Marcelo became a close friend and protector of Father Viader. This close friendship caused them to remain on the mission grounds where pale ghosts of two men have been seen together, floating or hovering outside the north wall of the old mission. Inside the church, people have experienced several cold spots. These may be ghosts of the mission Indians, hundreds of whom died there of white-man's diseases and the disintegration of their culture.

An American was killed there in 1846 during one of the skirmishes of the Bear Flag rebellion. The man was one of 175 Americans who set up barricades and other defenses around the mission to protect women and children from the advancing Mexican soldiers led by Don Francisco Sanchez. During a fearful night attack, the man died when his old, rusty gun blew up in his face.

CHAPTER 5

East Bay Area

The East Bay Area has a rich history, well-preserved in hundreds of Victorian mansions, old office buildings, hotels and resorts, wharves and docks, airplanes, boats, bars and cemeteries. Local Indians, Spanish explorers, Yankee sailors, writers, pirates, and fishermen have left an indelible mark on the land and a lingering echo of their lives that is easy to detect. The under-appreciated charms of Oakland, the excitement of Berkeley, and peaceful ambience of small towns such as Alameda and Clayton, provide a wide variety of ghost-hunting experiences.

CITY HALL PLAZA

Telegraph and Broadway between Fourteenth and Fifteenth Streets
Oakland, CA 94612-4011

Located in the heart of the City of Oakland, this beautiful plaza has been the site of several historical events and several sightings of ghostly phenomena. In the 1890s, many political events took place there that ended in riots and bloodshed. Rallies held by socialists, communists, and anarchists often attracted mounted police in addition to members of every fringe political group in the East Bay.

Political philosophers, such as Herbert Spencer, Frank Strawn-Hamilton, and the eighteen-year-old "boy socialist" Jack London, worked the crowds to frenzy with eloquent oratory and attacks on capitalism and the oppressive social order of the day. On occasion, the listeners sprang into action and marched through adjoining streets, disrupting commerce and damaging property. Police usually kept them in line with billy clubs and handcuffs. Heated emotions of the day may have caused some spirits of the revolutionists to remain in Oakland City Plaza, waiting for the day when socialism would overthrow capitalism.

The solitary oak tree in the center of the plaza has been the site of several sightings. One precipient has heard the shouts and screams of a riot and felt the rush of spirits as they flee to the north side of the plaza. Others, sitting on a bench in the quiet plaza, have been joined by pale images of people dressed in Victorian-era clothing. An elderly gentleman, in a tall hat, frequents the benches on the south side of the plaza. The ghost of a child in turn-of-the-century clothing has been seen on the east side. One precipient believes the child is searching for his father.

USS *HORNET*

Former Alameda Naval Air Station
Atlantic Avenue entrance
Alameda, CA 94501-1147
(510) 521-8448.

Haunted houses are almost cliché, but so are haunted ships. This is true of combat ships and other vessels that served in combat zones. The World War II haunted aircraft carrier, USS *Hornet,* is open to the public at the former Alameda Naval Air Station. She was commissioned on November 29, 1943, and sent to the South Pacific to avenge the lost of her namesake, the aircraft carrier *Hornet,* that was sunk by the Japanese in 1942 at Guadalcanal. Pilots flying from her deck sank seventy-three Japanese ships and destroyed 1,410 enemy aircraft. During the bloody battles of Okinawa and Iwo Jima, the *Hornet* came under heavy attack fifty-nine times. The last mission of this warship was a peaceful one, however. On July 24, 1969, she recovered the *Apollo 11* astronauts upon their return from the moon.

The nine-hundred-foot long ship was decommissioned in 1979 and sat many years awaiting restoration. It was during this time that caretakers began noticing strange sounds and other odd events. At times, when no other living soul was aboard the old ship, watchmen heard loud tapping sounds reverberating through the steel hull. Heavy steel doors would slam shut or swing open. The possibility that these events could result from movement of the ship was dismissed, for the

The aircraft carrier, USS Hornet, *docked in Alameda, is the home of several ghosts documented by ghost hunters for TV programs.*

42,000-ton vessel sat in placid, protected waters at Hunter's Point Naval Shipyard off of San Francisco. Wind and tide could not cause rocking or other motions of the huge ship.

The old *Hornet* opened as a museum in August of 1998. During restoration, the workers noticed the slamming doors and the sounds of footsteps on the metal deck. Since then, the *Hornet* has been visited by ghost hunters and psychics who detected several ghosts on board. The pilot's briefing room is often visited by ghosts of World War II aviators whose spirits returned to the ship after being shot down in the battle of Iwo Jima. Cold spots have been identified on the captain's bridge, the enlisted men's berthing areas, and the forward hangar deck on the starboard side of the ship. One percipient heard the sounds of a World War II aircraft landing on the deck.

LA COCOTTE RESTAURANT

6115 Main Street
Clayton, CA 94517
(925) 672-1330

In the 1880s, Clayton was a country town with little of the sophistication and civil disobedience that characterized the large cities on San Francisco Bay. Mining and ranching were the principle economic activities and the local population was largely transient and as wild as the countryside. On weekends, the bars were full of gamblers and drunks. Local peace officers stayed busy while the upstanding citizens stayed indoors with their heads down.

One late Saturday afternoon, two miners became involved in a heated argument inside a bar known as the Growler. Each packed a revolver. They became itchy for a gunfight as they traded insults and accusations. At last, one of the miners reached his limit. He pulled his gun and fired. He missed the other miner, but his bullet penetrated a wall and struck a little girl as she stood on Main Street. The bleeding child was taken inside the bar where the patrons attempted to save her life, but the wound was fatal. She died on the floor amid a crowd of miners full of sorrow over such a terrible accident.

Over the years, the Growler was sold to various people whose businesses failed in the old building. The place stood empty for many years, during which stories spread about cries and moans rising at times from the silence of the deserted barroom.

In the 1980s, while the building was undergoing renovation, strange red stains were discovered on the floor. Strong cleaning solutions and hard work removed them but they would soon reappear. Local ghost hunters believe these stains are remnants of blood from the wounds of the unlucky little girl. The frustrated owners of the building placed a carpet over the stains and opened for business.

Today, the old Growler bar is a popular French restaurant. Some visitors report seeing red stains on the floor while others have seen the little girl inside the restaurant or standing on Main Street where she was struck by miner's bullet 120 years ago.

THE OLD CRAFTS SHOP

Northeast corner of Center Street and Marsh Creek Road
Clayton, CA 94517

Sometime before World War II, a two-story building was constructed at this site. It served as a private residence and office with beautiful gardens, but no one lived there for more than a few years. By the 1970s, the place had been transformed into a commercial building. The second floor housed a craft shop with areas set up for sales and instruction. The ground floor was set aside for staff as a rest area.

By 1980, reports of several types of poltergeist activity began to circulate throughout the town. It was said that gusts of wind would pass down the halls even when all windows were shut. Locked doors were heard opening and slamming shut, and objects would fly off the walls. White figures were also seen there. Several psychics identified the spirits of native Americans in and around the building. They suspect that the place was built over an ancient Indian burial ground.

At the nearby creek, the ghost of an elderly lady in a rocking chair was seen on many occasions. Local history suggests that she is waiting for her daughter who drowned in the creek. Another tragedy occurred in front of the building around the turn of the century. A judge died when his buggy tipped over. These and other events contributed to a reputation for a bad atmosphere in and around the building.

In more recent times, the Utley family lived in an old craft shop. They experienced disembodied moaning, chairs that rocked without occupants, objects that flew from the walls nearly striking them, and a foreboding sense of evil. Local legend tells that bad things happened to children who lived there. Some became ill while others displayed antisocial behavior. The place was sold to the Eccbarian family who suffered many ill effects that were later attributed to evil spirits. They lost money on their business dealings while some family members went insane and the young people had severe behavior problems. A fire in the building burned many of their belongings while the walls were untouched by the flames. The old building was demolished soon after.

A modern building stands in the old craft shop's place, but many locals refuse to go in it. One percipient warns that the evil spirits at the site tend to latch onto residents and visitors, and attempt to destroy their lives. Young people are particularly vulnerable.

SATHER TOWER (THE CAMPANILE)

University of California campus
Telegraph Avenue at Bancroft Way
Berkeley, CA 94704.

Sather Tower, also known as the Campanile, was built in the 1950s. The observation deck, nearly two hundred feet above the ground, offers a magnificent view of the campus, the bay, and San Francisco. Its open portals also allow the wind to blow through the observation deck, creating a feeling of freedom and relaxation to many visitors. The Campanile also offers a way to make a speedy descent to the ground.

When the university switched its academic calendar from the relaxed, slow semester system to the frantic pace of the quarter system, some students joked that the Campanile's observation deck should be closed. The inference was that it offered a convenient suicide venue. These jokes persisted until a student did jump to his death in the mid-1960s. Soon after this tragic event, a woman reported that she had been followed by a ghost while walking across the grass on the west side of the Campanile. She was unable to give a description that matched that of the suicide victim. Others passing through the same area have also felt the presence of someone hovering close.

Local legend tells of a person who took a photograph of a hand reaching out from the grass. Similar sensations have been reported by visitors on the observation deck. One percipient sensed profound sadness and a longing for help.

NORTONVILLE CEMETERY AT BLACK DIAMOND MINE PRESERVE

100 Sommersville Road
Clayton, CA 94565
Clayton Historical Society: (925) 672-0240
www.ebparks.org

Noah Norton arrived in eastern Contra Costa country in 1855. Having considerable experience in the mining industry in Nova Scotia and Virginia, he founded a coal-mining operation, complete with a workers' village, company store, and modern machinery.

The place was home to several Welsh miners and their families. Living in the shadow of Mount Diablo didn't discourage these people from establishing a thriving community. Stories of spectral figures flying over the slopes of the strange mountain and sightings of the devil didn't scare them off. By 1885, however, the coal mine had played out and the village, named Nortonville in honor of its founder, lay deserted. All that remained were crumbling shacks, rusted machinery, and a rather full cemetery.

Life in Nortonville was hard for many folks, so survivors moved on, looking for a better life in the Bay Area, while the victims of coal-mine injuries, lung disease from coal dust, and infectious diseases that had rampaged through the small community were left in Rose Hill Cemetery.

Over the years, desecration of the graves and vandalism got to be too much for residents of the cemetery. Angry, unsettled spirits began harassing many visitors to the area. Hundreds have experienced poltergeist activity and ghostly, disembodied sobbing and laughter. Cold spots, brushes with spiritual entities, and the sound of bells tolling are common experiences for people in Nortonville.

More than one hundred exorcisms have been performed at the graveyard in an effort to settle some of the most malicious spirits. Almost everyone who visits the cemetery experiences a feeling of ghosts watching them or hovering close by. Some have left the area screaming with fright.

One of the ghosts of Nortonville's Rose Hill Cemetery has attained status as a local legend. Sarah Norton, also known as Granny Norton, served her community as a midwife from 1855 until her death on October 5, 1879. She died when her buggy tipped over as she raced to the nearby town of Clayton. The story tells of a sudden, strong wind that descended the slopes of Mount Diablo, frightening Granny's horse and tipping her buggy.

Granny had stipulated that there be no religious ceremony at her funeral, but people say that during the burial, a storm rolled through the area all of a sudden. From that time to the present, dark stormy nights are times when Granny's spirit is said to roam the area. In more recent years, Granny has become known as the White Witch because she wears a white gown and appears to have a pointed nose. Visions of the White Witch have been reported in the Oakland hills and several surrounding communities, as well.

Some of the residents of the town of Clayton dress up as Granny Norton on Halloween and her buggy ride is reenacted through the streets of Clayton. Some locals fear this angers Granny's spirit and results in more haunting activity around the cemetery.

CROLL'S BAR

Corner of Webster Street and Central Avenue
Alameda, CA 94501
Croll's Pizza Deli: (510) 865-6662

For over one hundred years, Croll's Bar was a popular drinking establishment for sailors, longshoremen, and fishermen residing in Alameda. The place opened in 1881 and closed in 1998. Many sailors, soldiers, and marines had their last drinks there before shipping out to foreign ports or combat zones of the Spanish-American War, WWI, WWII, Korea, and Vietnam. The bar's close proximity to the Alameda Naval Air Station made it a first stop for many of the military returning from those historic events.

Over the years, local legends developed about fights, robberies, and shootings that supposedly took place there. At various times, Croll's Bar was known as a very rough place on a Saturday night. There are no official records available confirming fatal shootings, but the eerie atmosphere of the place suggests that something bad happened there.

The bar was closed and sits vacant now. The laughter, music, and wild banter of the huge drinking crowd is still heard, though, by those sensitive people who visit the site. These sounds can be detected late in the evening at the threshold of the Webster Street entrance. They come as brief but unmistakable audible remnants of ghosts that still hang out at Croll's Bar. A dark figure is often seen standing in the doorway looking out to the street. This ghost may be waiting for long lost friends to return from a war so that can drink a few rounds at Croll's Bar.

Croll's 1883 bar, in Alameda, was a favorite drinking establishment for Navy sailors before shipping out.

HEINOLD'S FIRST AND LAST CHANCE SALOON

56 Jack London Square
Oakland, CA 94607-3700
(510) 839-6761

In the 1880s, the Oakland waterfront was a wild place. Ships came to call from all over the world. Their crews would hit the town with money in their pockets and lust in their hearts. Sailors, longshoremen, and naval personnel supported a bustling community of bars and brothels, and kept the jail full.

In 1880, the crew of a whaling ship was incarcerated so long that the ship was abandoned. The old vessel became grounded on the Oakland mud and soon local scavengers stripped her of wood, metal, and other valuable building materials. Much of her timber was used to build a solid structure that served three years as a boarding house for sailors.

The place was purchased by Johnny Heinold in 1883 for one hundred dollars and transformed into a bar. Johnny's bar became a popular waterfront gathering place for oyster pirates and the lawmen who pursued them on San Francisco Bay.

In the late 1880s, a boy named Jack London sat on the stool selling newspapers to patrons. Later, he sat at a corner table to do his schoolwork. Not only was young Jack London inspired by the exciting stories of adventure told by the men drinking at the bar, but at the age of sixteen, Jack made a deal to purchase his first sailboat while seated at a corner table.

In the 1920s, Johnny's bar became known as the First and Last Chance Saloon. The place stood at the foot of a pier from which ferryboats carried passengers to the dry town of Alameda. Johnny's bar was the last chance for a drink before passengers departed for Alameda and their first chance upon returning to Oakland.

Over the years, sailors, soldiers, marines, aviators, and others embarking on far reaching adventures have made Johnny's bar a last stop before departure, and a first stop upon returning home.

Many of these adventurers have returned only in spirit. The warped floorboards, century-old chairs, stools, and tables offer an

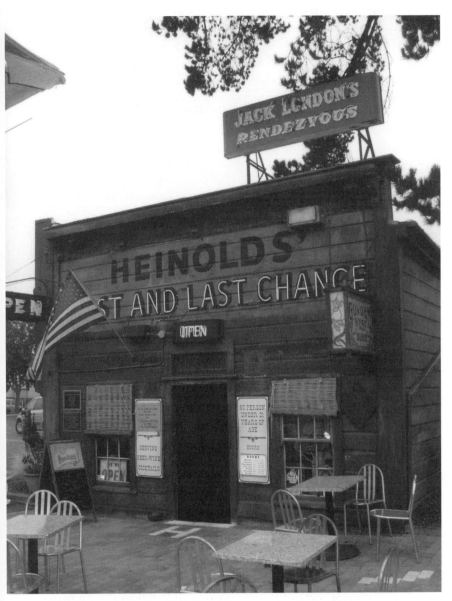

Jack London worked in this historic Oakland bar at the age of ten and took his first drinks here. His ghost still waits for the oyster pirates to join him for a nightcap.

atmosphere of timelessness that is comforting to the living as well as the dead. Some ghost hunters have sensed the spirit of Jack London and members of his oyster pirate gang. Others have experienced the touch of the long-departed Johnny Heinold. Several cold spots in the tiny bar could be the spirits of famous visitors from long past decades including Robert Louis Stevenson, Earle Gardner, Ambrose Bierce, Robert Service, and Joaquin Miller. The old photographs and other maritime souvenirs mounted on the walls document the history of this old bar and provide hints of the identity of the many spirits who still visit the First and Last Chance Saloon.

WESTERN AEROSPACE MUSEUM

Old Oakland Airport
8260 Boeing Street #621
Oakland, CA 94621-4544
(510) 638-7100

On a side street, off Earhart Road, aircraft sit, longing to take to the skies once again. Vietnam-era jet fighters and bombers, experimental aircraft, and a huge flying boat comprise part of a fascinating collection of historic aircraft, most of them restored to their former glory.

The Western Aerospace Museum opened in 1988, providing a home for several historic aircaft. The largest airplane is the Short Solent flying boat built in 1946. She is an upgraded passenger version of the successful World War II British *Sunderland* that searched for and sank German submarines in the north Atlantic. The four-engine *Solent* has a wing span greater than ninety feet and a tail that reaches thirty-seven feet above the ground. She was only able to take off and land in water. From the late forties to 1957, the *Solent* flew thirty-nine passengers in complete luxury from England to South Africa. Since the trip required a few days, passengers disembarked at stopover points and stayed in hotels situated near large bodies of placid water.

The *Solent* may be toured with a member of the museum staff. Several compartments display the luxury and style of the 1940s, an atmosphere conducive to making a psychic or spiritual connection with the past. In the rear of the aircraft, a lounge offers more than the ambience of 1940. One percipient has sensed the presence of an elderly woman there. She sits on the left side of the cabin, creating an atmosphere described as very dense and cold. Another ghost hunter has seen the pale apparition of a man dressed in a pilot's uniform. He stands in the doorway of the cockpit, watching people touring his aircraft.

Other aircraft at the museum may be haunted. While standing next to the A-4 jet fighter, one percipient sensed intense vibration and the sound of a jet engine.

PRESIDENTIAL YACHT, *POTOMAC*

540 Water Street
Oakland, Ca 94607-3746
(510) 839-7533

The USS *Potomac* was built in 1934 to serve as a Coast Guard cutter, and christened the *Electra*. In 1936, ignoring the maritime curse of bad luck for any vessel that is renamed, the Navy converted the

This presidential yacht was FDR's oasis from the pressures of running the country. After his death, the yacht was used by drug smugglers.

376-ton vessel to a presidential yacht for Franklin D. Roosevelt, and renamed her the *Potomac*. She had a long and glorious career as a presidential yacht without many spells of bad luck, but she did end up on the wrong side of the law at the bottom of San Francisco Bay.

Roosevelt used the yacht to meet with his closest advisors, entertain foreign dignitaries such as King George and Queen Elizabeth of England, and as a respite from the summer heat of Washington, D.C. Eleanor Roosevelt celebrated her fifty-seventh birthday on the yacht in 1941. After the president's death in 1945, the *Potomac* passed through private hands until she became involved in drug smuggling along the West Coast of the U.S. In 1980, she was seized by federal agents on San Francisco Bay, her hull was pierced and she sank off Treasure Island. After the Navy re-floated her, she was purchased by the Port of Oakland and restored to her former glory. The USS *Potomac* is now open to the public for tours and cruises on the Bay.

The spirits of at least three ghosts have been detected on the *Potomac*. In the engine room, percipients have sensed a man dressed in dark clothing, no doubt a sailor who operated the machinery. He doesn't seem to move about or make gestures with his hands. He merely stands as if awaiting orders from the bridge. In the forward crew's quarters, strange sounds plus humming and muted laughter, are often heard. One ghost hunter also experienced a profound sense of fear and sadness there. She feels this is related to the ship's days in the drug smuggling business.

On the fantail, the pale image of a short man dressed in a suit appears near the railing. He may have been one of FDR's political advisors. Perhaps he has returned to attend the president's cocktail parties staged there for FDR's closest friends and advisors.

PRESERVATION PARK VICTORIAN HOMES

1233 Preservation Park Way
Oakland, CA 94612
(510) 874-7580

In the late nineteenth century, Oakland was the second largest city in California. It was known for its thriving industries and as a commercial center of the state. Its citizens enjoyed great personal success amid the gentle climate and park-like atmosphere of old Oakland. They contributed to the general welfare of the city by establishing a public transit system, excellent public schools and academies, several parks, and paved streets. Oakland's residents also established magnificent neighborhoods in which the streets were lined with trees and nearly every home was surrounded by decorative fences and large gardens. Oakland was truly a land of oaks and other trees, and homes that reflected the success of its citizens.

Preservation Park serves as a fine example of old Oakland. This collection of sixteen Victorian homes is one of the finest in America. Five homes sit in their original locations while eleven others were moved from nearby neighborhoods to make way for a freeway. All of these beautiful buildings have been restored to their original grandeur. Several are open to the public, accessible by special tour, or available for parties or meetings.

The Remillard House offers an interesting history that connects a wealthy family with the region's most famous author. Pierre Remillard arrived in Oakland from Montreal in 1881. In just five years he rose from a hired hand to the wealthy owner of a brick manufacturing company. In 1887, he built a twenty-room mansion in the Queen Anne style. Pierre's daughter, Lillian, was popular among local high school students. She tutored many of them who struggled to learn the French language. Her most ardent student was a kid from a poor neighborhood. She enjoyed working with him because, in spite of his social position, he was well-mannered and highly disciplined in his study habits. His name was Jack London. Lillian and Jack spent many hours together in the parlor of the Remillard House studying French. In later years, he used this experience as a model for several passages in his novel, *Martin Eden.*

Lillian became the Countess Dandini and ran the family brick business until her death in 1963. Local ghost hunters have detected her presence on the porch of her magnificent mansion. Admirers of Jack London have searched the place for his ghost as well.

Other homes in Preservation Park are also believed to be haunted. Ghost hunters have investigated Nile Hall, built in 1911 as the Nile Social Club, and the James White House, built in 1875 by the founder of the Seventh Day Adventist Church. The ghost of a child playing with a stick and barrel ring has been seen by some visitors at the 1873 Latham-Ducel fountain.

CAMRON-STANFORD HOUSE

1418 Lakeside Drive
Oakland, CA 94612
(510) 444-1876

This ornate, Italian-style Victorian mansion is the last of many that once stood on the shores of Lake Merritt, named for the two most prominent families who occupied the house during the first thirty-one years it served as a private residence. Will and Alice Camron built the mansion in1876 and moved in for a brief stay in 1877. Later in the year, the family of David Hewes moved in and staged the biggest social event in the house's history. Franklina Hewes was married there late in 1877. Lucy Webb Hayes, first lady of the United States, was among her wedding guests. From 1881 to 1902 the mansion was home to Josiah Stanford, brother of Leland Stanford, who was governor of California in 1876.

In 1907, the City of Oakland bought the mansion and renovated it for use as a museum. It served in this capacity until 1967 when the new city museum opened nearby. The city then began a lengthy preservation process to restore the ornate house to its former glory as a home for some of Oakland's wealthiest citizens. Through the efforts of more than one thousand volunteers, artists, craftsman, and historians, the Camron-Stanford house regained the atmosphere of the 1880s. Sensitive visitors experience a time warp there now, and feel the texture of another age. Some of them also feel the presence of ghosts.

One ghost hunter who, as a child, frequented the old Oakland Museum, returned as an adult to confirm his suspicion that the ghost of a young woman haunts the place. At the tender age of twelve, he thought he saw a young woman descend the staircase and pass through the foyer, then disappear as she entered the parlor. The experience left an indelible mark on his memory. During his return visit many years later, the man encountered the ghost on the porch. He sensed that the young woman was waiting for someone to return home to this fascinating portal to the 1880s. Suspicions run high that this ghost is Franklina Hewes.

WHEELER OFFICE BUILDING

2409 Franklin Street
Oakland, CA 94612

For many years this busy but ordinary office building had a strange countenance about it. Local legend held that employees and visitors felt strange things, such as the sensation that they were being watched by an ethereal being. In 1964, the place gained national attention. Reports of violent poltergeist activity were made, including cabinets tipping over and telephones ringing without a caller. Objects flew off the wall, injuring some employees, and lights flashed on and off. The building's electrical system was inspected and every phone was replaced. Frightening poltergeist activity continued and reached such frightful levels that police were called. At last, an investigator from UC Berkeley found the cause of these strange happenings and offered a solution. Dr. Arthur Hastings determined that a young male employee had caused all of the disruption. It seems, without knowing it, he was evoking psychokinetic events as a result of personality conflicts he had with several employees in his office. The young man left the company and the psychokinetic events stopped.

A few weeks after the man's departure, some employees noted that the lights flashed on and off again, and objects disappeared only to reappear in strange places a few hours or days later. Historical investigation suggests that this building sits on an Indian burial ground. Percipients who enter the building feel a strangeness about the place and there is a sense of crowding as though several spirits are trying to block entry or push visitors out the door.

CLAREMONT RESORT AND SPA

41 Tunnel Road
Berkeley, CA 94705 510)
843-3000

Only a few of the thousands of "gold rushers" ever found their fortune in the streams and mines of California in 1849. One lucky man who struck it rich was a Kansas farmer named Bill Thornburg. He brought his wife and daughter to California with the promise that he would build the English castle his wife had always dreamed of having.

Bill found suitable land in the Bay Area and purchased thirteen thousand acres. He built a sprawling castle, stables, barns, training areas for pedigreed horses, and facilities for a large staff. Mrs. Thornburg's fascination of English society resulted in the marriage of her daughter to a British lord. After the daughter moved to England, Mrs. Thornburg became ill and died. Bill sold the property a few months later. On July 14, 1901, the castle burned to the ground along with several out buildings.

The land passed through the hands of many people before another successful gold seeker, Eric Lindblom, built a sprawling Mediterranean hotel after he struck it rich in the Alaska gold rush of 1898. His opulent hotel opened in time for the Panama-Pacific Exposition of 1915. Several renovation projects over the years have created a modern luxury resort that maintains the romantic style of Mrs. Thornburg's beloved castle. In fact, her ghost has been seen wandering the verandas and walkways of the Claremont Resort. Dressed in a Victorian gown, she glides around the gardens and seems quite pleased with the way her castle has been transformed into a beautiful hotel.

Local ghost hunters believe another female ghost haunts the terrace bar. In the 1930s, a law prohibited the sale of alcohol within one mile of the University of California. A young lady took it upon herself to measure the exact distance from the university to the front steps of the Claremont Resort. At the time, the Claremont did not have a bar because everyone assumed it fell within the one-mile limit, but she found that the Claremont was a few feet beyond. As a consequence, a bar was opened and the young woman was granted free drinks for life. She may be enjoying this reward at the terrace bar throughout her death, as well.

FACULTY CLUB AT UNIVERSITY OF CALIFORNIA

University Avenue
UC Berkeley campus
Berkeley, CA 94710
(510) 540-5678

The University of California at Berkeley boasts an academic

community that demonstrates intense loyalty. Members of the faculty tend to stay in their professorial positions for decades and retire as emeritus professors. Professor Henry Stephens came to UC in the 1890s to teach literature. Stephens lived in room 219 of the Faculty Club for about twenty years. He died in 1919 but his ghost remained in residence to enjoy the university community and continue his study of poetry and literature.

Many have seen his apparition sitting in a chair with a book on his lap. Some students, passing by his window, claim to have heard him recite poetry. In 1974, a visiting scholar from Japan reported seeing Professor Stephens' ghost sitting in his favorite chair. This reliable observer also reported seeing two heads floating across the room.

HIGHLAND GENERAL HOSPITAL

1411 East Thirty-First Street
Oakland, CA 94602
(510) 437-4800

Most hospitals harbor ghosts of deceased patients or spirits seeking loved ones who died of serious illnesses or injuries. After an unexpected death, these spirits are confused by the transition. They cannot understand that they have died. Some remain at the death site, trying to get the attention of loved ones or help from a stranger. Highland General Hospital has many of these ghosts. This medical center opened in the 1890s as the primary medical facility for the East Bay. Over the years, its buildings were remodeled, reconstructed, and supplemented by modern structures. The older parts of the medical center are easy to identify, though. They are the best places for sighting a ghost. The waiting areas near surgery, and the basement floor clinics and office areas, are good sites for ghost hunting, too.

It is best to visit these areas late in the evening prior to the end of visitor hours. Percipients have experienced intense cold spots and that eerie feeling that someone was looking over their shoulder or standing very close. One ghost hunter saw an old woman, dressed in black, in a waiting area on the basement level. She appears to be sobbing. Once, she turned to face the ghost hunter and said, "I hope he'll be all right." When asked to whom she referred, the old woman brought her handkerchief to her face and faded away.

CASA PERALTA

384 West Estudillo Avenue
San Leandro, CA 94577
(510) 577-3492

Don Luis Maria Peralta never dreamed that his service as a soldier, in one of the earliest explorations of California, would result in fame, fortune, and a lasting mark upon the East Bay's communities. In 1820, Don Luis was rewarded with forty-four thousand acres of land that comprises several East Bay cities now. Today, the name Peralta graces parks, streets, hills, schools, and other landmarks. Over the ensuing decades, Don Luis' lands were sold or given to relatives.

In 1874, Peralta's granddaughter, Ludovina Peralta, received land in the area known as San Leandro. By 1901, a nine-room, Victorian

The ghosts of two lovers, Antonio Martin and Hermina Peralta, may haunt this historic San Leandro home.

house stood on the property. Ludovina lived there with her sister, Maria, and a niece, Herminia Peralta. When Ludovina and Maria passed away, Herminia inherited the house and lands, and stayed there throughout her marriage to publisher William Dargie. When he died, Herminia traveled in Europe, gathering ideas for remodeling her home. She brought a dashing twenty-one-year-old architect from Spain, Captain Antonio Martin, to San Leandro in 1926 to transform her house into a Spanish estate.

Antonio Martin knocked out walls, created arched passageways, and added colorful Moorish tiles and decorative murals to parts of the house. When his work was completed, he remained in residence on the estate in a small apartment. There is no historical evidence, but many have speculated that Herminia and Antonio had quite a torrid affair. The fact that Herminia left her house and half her lands to him lends credence to the idea. Also, his apartment was a short distance across an elevated walk from the sunroom, one of Herminia's favorite parts of the house.

Added drama came after Herminia's death when her will was contested and Antonio lost all claim to the estate he had called home, due to bitter disputes with Herminia's relatives. Later, the land was sold in parcels and the house passed through the hands of several Peralta descendents. In the 1940s, Casa Peralta served as a hospital for treatment of alcoholism and later became a nursing home.

Today, Casa Peralta is restored and open for tours and special events. It is a fascinating museum depicting Herminia's life through displays of furniture, photographs, art, and clothing. Antonio's artistic and architectural additions to the house are highlighted as well.

Local ghost hunters believe that Antonio's ghost is still in residence at his beloved Casa Peralta. Perhaps he put so much of his soul into its architecture and art that his spirit could not let go of the place. He may have remained on the earthly plane to enjoy the place with Herminia, too, for the presence of a female spirit has also been detected there. Observers have seen the pale image of a small woman dressed in a Victorian gown in the garden and in a second floor bedroom. Other spirits, from the Casa's days as a hospital, may also inhabit the place.

CHAPTER 6

Locations Outside
the Bay Area

Within two hours' driving time of the Bay Area are many popular destinations for day trips or weekend getaways. Many of these locations, such as the gold rush Country and Monterey Peninsula, have a rich historical legacy preserved in old public buildings, houses, inns, cemeteries, ships, and numerous sites of historic events. These places offer great opportunities for ghost hunting. Check with a local visitor's bureau or historical society to get a map of historic sites and information about events such as special tours, festivals, and anniversaries of historical importance.

FIRE HOUSE MUSEUM GHOSTS

Fire House No. 2
Nevada County Historical Museum
214 Main Street
Nevada City, CA 95959-2509
(916) 265-5468

Like most of the ramshackle towns of the gold rush era, Nevada City was prone to fires that spread among the dry, wooden shacks and other buildings serving the somewhat transient population. The risk and fear of fire was so great, that citizens scrapped up the funds to build two firehouses. Fire House No. 1 was built at the lower end of the business district and serves today as a museum. This firehouse is an aging yet beautiful bell-tower structure of brick and wood decorated with Victorian gingerbread trim.

Several ghosts began to make their appearances on the first and second floors of the firehouse soon after gold rush era photos, furniture, and other historical items were moved into the building. Many visitors and employees have experienced cold spots and a sense of a thickened atmosphere. Some folks have heard footsteps when the building was deserted. Among the ghosts sighted there is a lady piano player from a local whorehouse and a lady dressed in neat Victorian attire who rummages through cabinets. Several visitors have seen a group of Chinese men standing about a thousand-year-old Taoist shrine, a remnant from the Chinese who helped build the railroads and bridges and worked in the mines.

SQUIRE WILLIAMS AND THE LADY IN GRAY

Red Castle Inn Bed and Breakfast
109 Prospect Street
Nevada City, CA 95959
(916) 256-5135

Standing across Highway 49 from the once wild gold-rush town of Nevada City is a magnificent brick mansion known as the Red Castle. The stately old place stands amid a thick grove of trees on a hillside, giving the appearance of being separate, not only from the town and its rush of tourists, but also from the modern age. Today, the Red Castle is a popular bed and breakfast that hosts many visitors who come to experience the ghosts of the gold rush era.

The four-floor mansion was built in 1860 by John Williams, a businessman from Illinois who had made a modest fortune in the gold fields and acquired the title Squire Williams. His large family, including his wife Abigail, his children, and many foster children, enjoyed the spacious home for many years until John died at the age of sixty-eight, on February 8, 1871. Three years later, John's eldest son, Loring, also died in February. Loring's will directed that his funeral be held on the same day of the week and at the same time of day as his father's. With the men of the house gone, Loring's wife, Cornelia, and his mother, Abigail, were left to carry on. When the frail Cornelia died on June 18, 1883, the real work began for the aristocratic Abigail. But after eight years of struggling to keep the mansion and her financial affairs in order, she sold the place in 1891 and moved to Southern California.

Throughout the 1870s and 1880s, the many children and foster children housed on the upper floor of the Red Castle were under the supervision of a governess. Her name is lost to history, but she is known to many ghost hunters as "the Lady in Gray." Her ghost and the ghost of John Williams are the two most often sighted. John Williams' ghost appears as an old, bearded man, dressed in a black frock coat and sometimes a tall hat. He has appeared during various periods of reconstruction of his beloved mansion, as if to inspect the work being done. Another gentleman in a hooded robe has been seen passing through the parlor on the second floor.

The most active ghost of the Red Castle Inn is the Lady in Gray, so named because she wears a gray Victorian gown. Many visitors have even heard her speak. She has carried on conversations with guests of the inn and burst into rooms searching for the children entrusted to her care. Many have heard the voices of girls and boys on the top floor where the children were housed. One man heard a boy say, "They're going into our room," as he entered a guestroom.

The magnificent parlor on the second floor is a good place to begin a ghost hunt. Not only was it the site of many happy occasions for the Williams family, but it served as the venue for the funerals of John, Loring, and Cornelia. Its antique furniture and wall hangings block out the influence of this century and seem to open a welcoming door for the many ghosts who cannot leave the Red Castle.

THE SENATOR AND HIS DAUGHTER

Sutter Creek Inn and B
75 Main Street
Sutter Creek, CA 96585
(916) 267-5606

In 1860, after the wild years of the gold rush, John Keyes settled in the rich little town of Sutter Creek. Nestled in the Sierra foothills, Sutter Creek was a perfect blend of excellent climate, accessible transportation to Sacramento, booming economy, and a developing society of gentle people. Most of the itinerant prospectors, trouble-makers, drunks, and highwaymen were gone by then and in their place came men like John Keyes. Mr. Keyes arrived in Sutter Creek late in 1859, eager to build a house for Miss Clara McIntyre, who would soon arrive from New Hampshire to become his bride. Anticipating Clara's homesickness, he built her a sprawling New-England-style cottage in 1860, to which he added even more rooms as the years passed by. Their life together was short and marred by the death of their only child from diphtheria. Not long after that, John died, making Clara a widow at the age of thirty-four.

Being alone, yet well-established in Sutter Creek, Clara was much sought after by suitors, one being State Senator Edward C. Voorhees. Edward won her hand on March 29, 1880, in a ceremony in the rose garden behind Clara's house. The house passed to their daughter, Gertrude, in later years. She sold it before departing for a nursing home, and then the great beyond. Jane Way converted the charming house to an inn and that's when the ghosts appeared.

The first to appear was a stately-looking gentleman in a dark suit and tall hat. He appeared one evening as Jane was preparing to go out to a party, and announced, "I will protect your inn." Later, Jane saw an old photograph of Senator Voorhies and realized that it was his ghost who had returned to the Sutter Creek cottage. Some time later, the senator's daughter, Gertrude Voorhies, appeared. Moving about the parlor, Gertrude's ghost inspects the furniture and decorations to see if her beloved home is being maintained in a proper manner.

Guests at the inn don't seem to be bothered by these ghosts. Indeed, many visitors come to the inn seeking an experience with the ghosts of Edward and Gertrude, or any of the other ghosts who roam about the quaint old town of Sutter Creek.

THE LADY IN BURGUNDY

Pioneer Graveyard
Cold Springs Road near Highway 49
Coloma, CA 95613

Cold Springs Road winds around the wooded hills of Coloma in the Sierra Nevada Mountains, past several historical sites and buildings left from the gold rush days. As the road descends through the scattered community toward the American River, it separates the haunted Vineyard House Inn from Coloma's Pioneer Cemetery. Among those seeking rest there are miners, prospectors, explorers, farmers and their families, murderers, and a few hookers. It is also the resting place of Robert and Louise Chalmers, owners of the Vineyard House built in the 1870s, and two men executed in front of that house on makeshift gallows. Motorists passing by in both daylight and at night have reported a mysterious woman standing at the roadside, beckoning them to turn into the cemetery for a visit.

Those who have seen the ghost agree that she appears in a burgundy dress. This is a remarkable report since most ghosts appear in black and white or in very muted colors. The woman's rosy cheeks are framed by black hair and she appears to be quite frantic or upset as she waves to passersby, trying to get them to stop. Some have described the swishing sound of her skirts as she turns away from the road before disappearing. She often makes direct eye contact with her piercing dark eyes, causing many locals to avoid passing the cemetery when they are alone at night.

Who is this mysterious lady in burgundy? The only clue is that she watches over one gravesite in particular. The plot contains the remains of Charles Schieffer, who died in 1864 at the age of forty-two; his son, William, who died in 1861 at the age of two years twenty-eight days; and daughter, May, who departed this world in 1890 at the age of twenty-seven. The grave of Catherine Schieffer, born in 1862 and died in 1916, lies in a distant section of the cemetery. Perhaps she was May and little William's sister, and Charles' daughter. Catherine may be the mysterious lady in burgundy who beckons from the roadside to visit her beloved father, sister, and brother. It is also possible that this ghost is the wife of Charles Schieffer. Perhaps she has forsaken her own grave, located elsewhere, and taken up residence near the resting place of her family.

Whoever the ghost is, the lady in burgundy is one of the most often observed ghosts in the gold rush country.

THE VINEYARD HOUSE

530 Cold Springs Road
Coloma, CA 95613
(916) 622-2217

Nestled in the rolling hills surrounding the historic gold-rush town of Coloma, the Vineyard House is one of the most haunted buildings in California. The large four-story building was constructed in 1879 by Robert and Louise Chalmers as an inn and restaurant, and has served as the site of several tragedies and the final home of many souls. Louise arrived in Coloma in the 1850s as the fourteen-year-old wife of a former gold-seeker, Martin Allhoff. Martin used his modest bag of gold to establish the winery and vineyards that later gave the inn its name. The wine business was profitable for many years, but certain financial irregularities led Martin into a state of depression and anxiety, causing him to commit suicide in Virginia City, Nevada, in 1866. His body was returned to Coloma and he now lies in the Pioneer Graveyard across the street from the crumbling remains of his dream, the Allhoff Winery.

This unhappy turn of events left Louise a widow with considerable business interests and valuable land. An astute suitor, Robert Chalmers, left his marginally successful hotel business in the Sierra, courted Louise, and married her in 1869. Relishing his new opportunity for success, he set about to improve the winery, adding another stone aging cellar in 1875 and planting additional acreage with grapes.

In 1879, Robert re-entered the hotel business when he and Louise opened the Vineyard House. Before long, the inn became the center for social activity in Coloma. Dignitaries visiting the area, including former president Ulysses S. Grant and writer Mark Twain, would consider lodging and dining only at the renowned Vineyard House. After all, its splendid ballroom, restaurant, and comfortable rooms were among the finest the gold rush country offered. But only two years after the grand opening, tragedy once again visited Louise.

Robert began to lose his memory, control of his speech, and his eyesight. His behavior progressed from being odd to violent. Louise was so frightened that she had a cell constructed in the basement in which she confined Robert until his death in 1881. Throughout his final days, Robert told friends that his illness was the result of his wife's efforts to poison him. Some historians believe he suffered from syphilis, but to others his symptoms and behavior suggest Alzheimer's disease. Robert is buried in the Pioneer Graveyard, but his ghost walks the halls of his inn.

Alone once again, Louise struggled to keep the business going but she fell into one difficulty after another. Later, the wine cellars were deeded to the State of California while the inn was sold to the son of Martin Allhoff after a series of legal suits that exhausted Louise. She died in 1900 in Los Angeles, but she rests next to Robert in the graveyard, at a site that offers a view of her beloved Vineyard House.

Today, the Vineyard House is a popular country inn and restaurant. It remains the social center of Coloma but also attracts people from all over the U.S., many of whom come for the ghostly activity for which the old inn is so well known. Among its ghosts are Robert and Louise, various prisoners who once occupied the basement cell prior to their execution in front of the inn, a two-year-old child, noisy gentlemen dressed in Victorian attire, a piano player, and a gambler.

Ghostly activity includes glasses that move across the surface of the bar, wall hangings that move without apparent cause, the sounds of rustling skirts, footsteps in the narrow halls, laughing men, screaming murder victims, and full apparitions. Among the latter are a two-year-old boy named George who died in the house and makes his appearances in the restaurant, and the stern-faced, bearded Robert Chalmers. Robert appears in the guest rooms, looking after patrons of the inn with a critical eye that unnerves some visitors. Sensitive people also feel his presence in the jail cell located in the basement that now serves as a popular bar. Occasionally spirits are rowdy and boisterous, filling the darkened hallways with their laughter and shouts. The most frightening spirits emit blood-curdling screams and create such a disturbance in a room on the upper floor that one couple dashed from their room in the middle of the night, thinking they had heard a murder occur in the adjacent room.

Ghostly activity has been experienced at the Vineyard at virtually every hour of the day or night throughout the year. Hot spots for observing ghostly activity are the jail cell in the bar, the restaurant, parlor, and the hallway of the upper floor. Halloween is a special time at the Vineyard House. Costumed guests obtain reservations a year in advance and share in an adventurous night of spook hunting and time travel to Coloma's Gold Rush Era.

PACHECO PASS—BLOOD ALLEY

Highway 152 East; from Gilroy to Interstate 5

This modern highway is a major link connecting the southern Bay Area and Monterey region with I-5 that runs from northern to southern California. The haunted section of 152 East starts in Gilroy, where it intersects Highway 101, and extends eastward forty-two miles to I-5. It is a heavily traveled road. In the past ten years, 169 people have lost their lives in traffic accidents on the tight curves and along the lonely stretches of a dangerous highway the locals call "Blood Alley."

Many of the ghost sightings and paranormal phenomena reported in connection with Highway 152 are attributed to those who lost their lives while driving through Pacheco Pass. Phenomena reported by tourists, truck drivers, and even the renowned psychic, Sylvia Brown, include odd, human-like sounds emanating from the back seat of an automobile, apparitions appearing in passenger seats, ethereal hitch-hikers, strange clouds flowing along the road's surface, and sudden flashes of light. One driver felt that control of his car had been taken over by an invisible force, possibly that of a spirit who had once lost control of his own car, and his life. Upon leaving a particular hazardous stretch of road, control of the car was returned to the stunned driver whose life might have been saved by the more experienced spiritual motorist.

Sylvia Brown investigated the Pacheco Pass section of Highway 152 East for the television program *Sightings*. She saw mounted cavalry riding near the road, covered wagons, faces of desperate people, and felt powerful energies from distant periods of history. It was explained that Pacheco Pass is a place where time is warped, allowing scenes and events from other times to appear in the present.

Other explanations focus on the role Pacheco Pass played in the movement of early settlers into the region, battles with local Indians and U.S. soldiers mounted on horseback. A look at a map of the region suggests another possibility—the highway cuts through mountains named the Diablo Range. Diablo is the Spanish word for devil. This ominous name has led some people to wonder if Pacheco Pass cuts through ground occupied by evil spirits.

MURPHYS HOTEL

459 Main Street
PO Box 329
Murphys, CA 95247
(209) 728-3444

Built in 1856, this hotel and bar retains the gold rush era atmosphere conducive to ghost hunting. Iron shutters that adorn the side windows still show bullet marks from the wild days of Murphys' past.

Many famous guests checked in there. The list includes Ulysses S. Grant, Mark Twain, Horatio Alger, and Charles Bolton, otherwise known as Black Bart. That gentleman bandit made Murphys Hotel his base of operations for many stagecoach robberies in the 1870s. He liked the place so much that he never checked out. Black Bart's ghost still roams the hallway on the second floor, seen as a dark, shadowy figure, often a full-bodied apparition. The bar at Murphys Hotel looks just as it did in 1856. At times, people notice cold spots at the end of the bar nearest the street.

Several other gold-rush buildings in Murphys are good places for haunting spirits. The general store across the street from the Murphys Hotel has an eerie atmosphere. You can visit nearby Mercer Caverns for an underground experience where at least one cave explorer died many years ago. The Stevenot Winery, two miles outside of Murphys, has an old barn where a local Indian was hanged by a crowd of angry pioneers.

BRICK HOTEL

Byron Hot Springs Road
Byron, CA 94514

Discovery Bay Chamber of Commerce
PO Box 658
Byron, CA 94514
(925) 634-9902

Clayton Historical Society
6101 Main Street
Clayton, CA 94517
(925) 672-0240

In the late 1860s, an elegant hotel was established in Byron as a hot
springs resort for wealthy ranchers and visitors from the Bay Area. The
waters had healing powers and comfort for those with arthritis and
other ailments. The hotel flourished for many years but the depression
of the thirties brought with it a decline in visitors and in 1938 the
resort was closed. The Brick Hotel sat unused for decades, falling apart
as the old mortar loosened and vandals knocked down walls.

Long before the resort closed, stories grew about the ghost of an
Indian maiden who walked the halls. Reports are that she was peaceful but guests were still shaken by the sight of her.

In recent years, local teenagers have gathered at the ruins of the
Brick Hotel and told ghost stories. Legends and stories about the
Indian maiden say that she was no doubt a member of a tribe that
used the hot springs as a site for religious activities. To this day, she
walks the halls and grounds of the old Brick Hotel, keeping watch
over a place that was sacred to her people.

THE CUSTOM HOUSE

At the foot of Fisherman's Wharf
Monterey, CA 93940-2806
(408) 649-7118 (Old Monterey Business Association)

Monterey is one of the most historical cities in the West.
Established in 1776, many government buildings, private homes,
places of worship, and sites of commercial activity from the Spanish
(1776-1820) and Mexican (1820-1849) periods remain well-preserved

and open to visitors. In addition, many ghost hunters visit old sites from the famous Cannery Row and the shipwreck locales.

Built of adobe in the 1820s, the Custom House sits at the foot of Fisherman's Wharf overlooking the former anchorage for sailing ships from Spain, Portugal, England, Mexico, and the East Coast that arrived after the arduous passage around Cape Horn to the distant outpost of early California. Until about 1860, the Custom House was the economic hub of California, receiving goods and passengers from every ship entering the region. Later, the place was rented to various entrepreneurs as a residence or place of business. These undocumented residents could well be a basis for reports of ghostly activity.

Among the sounds reported by visitors are footsteps, deafening rattles, swishing sounds from the walls, and creaking doors. In addition, several cold spots tend to move from room to room.

Apparitions include a gentleman and a boy who claim to have been murdered in the building. It seems the gentleman has complained to living persons that he was killed for his gold and buried with the boy near the stairs that lead to the tower. The graves have never been found, but locals believe the man still haunts the Custom House, awaiting the help of someone who would find his grave and give him a proper Catholic burial.

Over the years, ghosts have tried to rid the place of residents. One resident was tossed out of bed three times in one night by spirits who did not want him there. Some ghosts express their displeasure with tourists by creating areas of cold air or thick atmosphere that lend a sense of foreboding.

The Custom House may be home to several other lost souls who died thousands of miles from home in a country that was, at the time, on the other side of the world. The building, now part of the State Historical Park System, is a popular tourist spot. The best time for ghost hunting at the Custom House is during the first hour in the morning when there are few tourists. Another good time is late at night. The doors are locked at 5 A.M. but the quiet ambience surrounding the building creates the perfect setting for ghost hunting. After 9 A.M. few tourists are around and the lights of Monterey's harbor cast a warm glow upon the old adobe walls and veranda, creating an inviting atmosphere for the spirits who live in old Monterey.

ROYAL PRESIDIO CHAPEL

Church Street at Figueroa
Monterey, CA 93940-7806
(408) 649-7118 (Old Monterey Business Association)

Early in the Spanish Period (1776-1820) a presidio was established at Monterey to protect the region from foreign interlopers. An essential part of the military facilities was the Royal Presidio Chapel built in 1790. Its dim sanctuary offers many dark corners where spirits may rest, protected by thick adobe walls from the noise and light of the modern world.

Mass was said in the chapel weddings, baptisms, funerals, and other religious ceremonies for those who served the Spanish Crown in the remote colony of California.

The chapel was the seat of religious devotion and focal point for many people who lived half a world away from their homes and families in Europe. As such, the spirits of some of these early Californians still occupy the Royal Presidio Chapel.

Several visitors to the chapel have reported a bright candle that moves in the darkness throughout the sanctuary. Many solitary visitors have heard the sound of footsteps on the tile floor. On occasion, the swishing of skirts is heard moving up and down the central aisle. Sometimes people have heard the soft humming sound of priests or choir members chanting.

The most dramatic ghostly activity at the chapel occurs outside the building at night where the tower bells are heard at times when no one is pulling the ropes. Local ghost hunters believe an old Mexican servant who worked for the chapel priests remains to perform the honored duty left undone by the departed fathers of the Royal Presidio Chapel.

STOKES ADOBE

Hartnell Street at Calle Principal
Monterey, CA 93940

Built in the 1830s and standing near Colton Hall, the Stokes adobe is one of the best-preserved buildings from the Mexican period. The place was designed as one of the most luxurious homes in Monterey and, as such, it was the site of many important social events. Like so many of Monterey's adobes, the Stokes house served as home to several families over the years as well as a place for various businesses. Today, it is occupied by one of Monterey's best restaurants.

Ghostly activity in the Stokes adobe occurs late at night when the place is quiet. Footsteps are sometimes heard from the second floor and, on the first floor, the whimpering of a child has been reported. Lights seem to go off or on without explanation. Some visitors to the men's restroom have experienced an eerie feeling of someone looking over their shoulder.

COLTON HALL

Pacific Avenue between Jefferson and Madison streets
Monterey, CA
(408) 646-3851

Built in 1849, and named for the first American mayor of Monterey, Reverend Walter Colton, Colton Hall served as the meeting hall for the California constitutional convention. The two-story building has also been a school and courthouse. Today, the second floor is a museum. The front porch was used many times as a place for public hangings. In the 1860s, a vigilante committee took a prisoner from the nearby jail and hung him after they cleared the children from the Colton Hall School. Several others have been executed in front of Colton Hall and some locals believe ghosts remain there, demanding justice from those who pass by their death site.

Behind Colton Hall is the town jail. This stone building, constructed in 1854, served Monterey until 1956. The place is a veritable fortress from which no one ever escaped except by death. Legend holds that several inmates killed themselves during incarceration there.

HIGHWAY ONE AT MONASTERY BEACH

1.5 miles south of the intersection of Highway One and Rio Road
Carmel, CA

Just over the hill from Monterey lies Carmel. Beyond that little town, Highway 1 runs south along one of the most beautiful coastlines in the world. A mile and a half from the edge of town sits a crescent-shaped beach known as Monastery Beach. The place got its name from Carmelite Monastery that sits on the eastside of the highway. Built in 1925, the castle-like structure rests among the pine trees overlooking the coast. Motorists passing by at night have taken evasive action to avoid hitting a ghostly figure of a woman who crosses the two-lane road separating the monastery from the beach. She seems to cross the road without concern for passing cars or her safety. There is no information about her identity or why she remains near Monastery Beach and the Carmelite Monastery.

DOC RICKETT'S LAB

Cannery Row
Monterey, CA 93940
(831) 372-8512 (Cannery Row Foundation)

Just down the street from the famous Monterey Bay Aquarium is a squatty, weathered, wooden building with a warped staircase leading to the second floor. John Steinbeck made this structure famous as lab of marine biologist Doc Ricketts in the novels *Cannery Row* and *Sweet Thursday.* The forlorn lab sits among the bustling businesses of a revitalized Cannery Row. In the days of Steinbeck and Ricketts, the lab was the scene of all-night drinking sessions and riotous parties.

The place is open to the public only three days per year: John Steinbeck's birthday (February 27), Ed Ricketts' birthday (May 14), and during the Sardine Festival (early June). On other days of the year, visitors may climb the stairs to the front door and savor the essence of two of Cannery Row's most famous inhabitants.

The best time to soak up the atmosphere of spirits on Cannery Row is very late at night when the street is deserted. At these hours, visitors can experience the sounds, smells, and even a few apparitions of long-departed fisherman and cannery workers.

DOC RICKETTS' DEATH SITE

Wave Street on Cannery Row east end, at the intersection of the bike
  path
Monterey, CA 93940

On December 8, 1948, Ed Ricketts drove his old Buick out of the garage under his lab and headed down Cannery Row toward central Monterey. It was after 5 P.M. and Ed was hungry for a steak dinner. As he drove down the street, his mind wandered to the many pressing problems he faced. Changes in the local fishing industry and difficulties keeping his marine biology business going were worrisome to him. As Wave Street curved to the right, he turned his big Buick without thinking about it. He pressed on the accelerator a little more and proceeded up the inclined street into the path of the evening Del Monte Express. Ed's car was crushed by the huge train but the impact didn't kill him. He lingered for forty-eight hours before "giving up the ghost."

Everyone on Cannery Row was devastated by Doc Ricketts' death. He had been such a prominent character on the Row that his passing did, indeed, signal the end of an era. Ed not only achieved fame in Steinbeck's books, *Cannery Row* and *Sweet Thursday,* but also in Steinbeck's non-fiction book, *The Sea of Cortez.* Ed, the original party animal of Cannery Row, was kind to everyone, and generous with his beer and money. Doc, as he was known to his friends, was the heart and soul of Cannery Row.

Just as everyone on the Row loved Doc, he loved the Row. Many fans of Steinbeck's books have become fans of Doc. These people leave flowers and other gifts around the statue that marks the site of Doc's fatal accident. Others hold vigils late at night, savoring the essence of the hour as they try to tune into the old days on the Row. The anniversary of Doc's tragic accident is an important time for getting in touch with the spirit of the Row and the spirit of Doc Ricketts.

One percipient has heard the sound of the Del Monte Express as it rumbled down the track, crossing Wave Street. The old railroad right-of-way is now a bicycle path but the former position of the tracks is clearly marked. Several people have noted a cold spot that moves around the site but remains in the former path of the Del Monte Express. No one has reported the apparition of Doc Ricketts, but the cold spots may indicate that his ghost is trying to escape the on-coming train.

CHRISTIAN CHURCH OF LAKEPORT

Corner of Main Street and Sweet Street
Lakeport, CA 95453 (Clear Lake)

The age of this structure is unknown. It presently stands deserted due to many strange things that have been witnessed by several people since the late 1950s. Some time in the mid-1950s, a caretaker's arm was severed by a saw that someone had tampered with. The man died from his injury and he has been haunting the building ever since. Many believe he has been seeking revenge. In 1968, a man died while painting the steeple. His death occurred under suspicious circumstances. Children and adults who have entered the building have been frightened by strange noises, including the slamming of cabinet doors and rattling of windows. Others have described events here as a "reign of terror."

The most recent attempts to use the building failed after a short time due to haunting activities that disturbed the new owner. Reports say that the caretaker's ghost has taken up residence in the steeple and he is unhappy with intruders.

RED, WHITE, AND BLUE BEACH

Six miles north of Santa Cruz on Highway 1
(stop at the red, white, and blue mailbox)

This popular nudist beach is also accessible to clothed visitors, especially in the early evening when the air becomes chilly. A wooden house, built in 1857 by a retired sailor, and a campground are adjacent to the beach. It seems that the old sailor strolls out the back door of the house to make his rounds through the campground, and then on to the beach. There are times when the sailor appears upset by the state of affairs around his home. Visitors have reported seeing objects fly in their direction as if thrown by an invisible being. Even so, this ghost likes the beach kept clean. Empty soda cans often take flight in the direction of the trashcans.

Other spirits may haunt this beach. In 1986, a psychic and ghost hunter witnessed a thick fog rolling onshore from the ocean. Moments later, a huge black bird hovered over her head, then she felt an evil presence surround her. This experienced ghost hunter reported she was "scared to death."

DEL MONTE BEACH

The beach extends for three to four miles
East from the commercial fishing pier of Monterey
Del Monte Beach lies parallel to Del Monte Avenue

This long, wide beach is often covered with fog that seems to close out the modern world. At any time of day or night, when the fog rolls in, ghosts emerge to walk the sandy shores of Monterey Bay, one of the few places in California where multiple ghosts have been seen at the same time. As many as six full-bodied ethereal forms have appeared along the beach. No doubt these are the ghosts of people who lost their lives in the waters of Monterey Bay. For almost 150 years, Del Monte Beach has been a popular swimming and bathing site. At times, the surf runs high and dangerous currents create unseen dangers for swimmers and those wading in the shallows. Several people have drowned and many offshore accidents—from storms, shipboard fires, and other spooky events—have added to the list of those who lost their lives near Del Monte Beach.

A young woman dressed in a Victorian-Era bathing suite visited one ghost hunter as he sat upon the beach, gazing at boats offshore. Sensing a presence to his left, he turned to see a nearly transparent figure of a woman sitting next to him. She asked, "Where am I?" Then the image disappeared.

FISHERMEN'S WHARF

Del Monte Avenue
Monterey, CA 93940

Several visitors to the wharf have reported seeing ghosts of old fishermen. Typically, these ghosts sit on benches gazing out to sea as if pondering the return of their bodies. Some of them have spoken when spoken to. No specific identification of any of these ghosts has been made. Over the one hundred years that this wharf has been in use, countless fisherman and boatmen have departed the safety of their moorings only to lose their lives at sea. There have been fatal accidents on this pier, as well.

The best time to hunt for ghosts on Fishermen's Wharf is late at night when the businesses have closed and there are no fishermen around. Ghost hunters will experience a presence, then discover a grizzled old fisherman sitting next to them.

THE STONE CHURCH AND GRAVEYARD AT ROCKVILLE

Suisun Valley Road
1 mile north of intersection with Rockville Road
(in the Fairfield area, 94534; take I-80 East from the Bay Area; turn off on Suisun Valley Road heading north)

In 1852, settlers in the region held church services on the banks of Suisun Valley Creek and performed baptisms in the deep pools under shady oaks. By 1856, enough money was raised to build a simple but beautiful church using stone quarried from surrounding hills, hence the name Rockville. The church and adjacent cemetery were established on five acres donated by Landy and Sarah Alford. One of its first clergy was the Reverend Orcenith Fisher, known as the "Son of Thunder" because the stone walls of the church amplified his strong voice.

As expected, the Stone Church was the site of some sad events over the years. In 1863, the congregation was split by the Civil War with northern sympathizers leaving to worship elsewhere. A stone plaque, still visible, was erected by southern sympathizers marking the church as "Methodist Episcopal Church South."

The saddest event, however, was the passing of the Alfords' three-year old-daughter. Her beautifully carved stone marker is a focal point of the cemetery and still lends a tragic air to the place. Also interned there is Granville P. Swift, a member of the Bear Flag Revolt

The congregation of the Stone Church in Rockville was split by the Civil War. Ghosts of local pioneers appear in the adjacent graveyard.

that took place in Sonoma in 1846. Swift died on April 21, 1875, a week short of his fifty-fourth birthday, when he fell from his horse while prospecting in the nearby Suisun hills.

Today the Rockville Stone Church is a pioneer monument. Among the spirits who linger under the shady oaks to reside close to their beloved stone church is the partial apparition of Granville Swift. Some ghost hunters have seen him on horseback while others report seeing only his shoulders and head as he fades into the sunlight filtering through the trees near his grave.

CHIEF SOLANO BURIAL GROUNDS

1.5 miles south of Rockville on Suisun Valley Road
From the Bay Area, take I-80 east to Fairfield area, turn off on Suisun Valley Road, go about one mile north toward Rockville 94534.

About one mile from the village of Rockville lies a piece of ground that, prior to 1840, was the site of an Indian village occupied by Suisun Indians. The village, or *rancheria*, was spread over several hundred acres, including the boulder-strewn knolls that surround the area. Some of these boulders still bear the marks American Indians created in the process of grinding seeds and acorns. Most of the old rancheria is now part of Rockville Park. The suspected burial ground is bisected by Suisun Valley Road at a point where it passes Solano Community College and the old stone house erected in 1849 by the Martin family.

Near the road a buckeye tree stands, marking the spot where Chief Solano was buried. It is not known how many Indians are buried in the area, but it is likely that over a period of two of three centuries several hundred were put to rest there. None of them are honored by grave markers or historical plaques. This spot, nestled against the bluffs that form Rockville Park, a popular site for hiking and riding mountain bikes, was once a thriving Indian community as well as the site of a massacre. In 1810, Spanish troops, under Lt. Gabriel Moraga killed men, women, and children in the rancheria and took several children as slaves. One was a ten-year-old boy named Sina. He was taken to Mission Dolores in San Francisco, converted to Catholicism, and as an adult was renamed Francisco Solano. Standing six feet seven inches tall, he returned to the Suisun Indian villages and became their chief. In 1860, Solano died of pneumonia near the Martin's stone house. They buried him on their property, near a Buckeye tree under a cairn of stones. Over time, Solano's actual gravesite was lost. The Martin's publicly claimed that in the process of farming their property, stones were moved, leaving no monument to a great chief. Some local historians suspect that Solano's body was removed by local Indians, with the cooperation of the Martins, and buried in a secret place on the old rancheria.

A few locals have reported seeing partial apparitions of Chief Solano standing next to the Buckeye tree as they drive by the burial grounds in the evening. He does not present a menacing appearance, but gives the impression that he will not allow visitors to walk over the burial ground. One Rockville resident has seen the ghost several times. She describes him as very tall and slim with several feathers tied in his hair. He raises a hand where cars pass by, as if to indicate that they should not enter the burial ground.

The 1810 massacre site lies within Rockville Park. Local ghost hunters have frequented this place searching for the tortured souls of local Indians killed by the Spanish. When Lieutenant Moraga's troops entered the village on horseback, a local chief, Malica, and several braves took up defensive positions in a hut. The Spanish burned the hut, killing all of those inside. One local ghost hunter located a large cold spot near the grinding stones and detected other discreet local atmospheric changes that may indicate the former location of the hut where several brave men died. He has also detected a profound sense of terror and sadness at the site.

NEW HELVETIA; SUTTER'S FORT

Sutter's Fort State Historic Park
2701 L Street
Sacramento, CA 95814
(916) 445-4422

The spirit of the old west lives on at Sutter's Fort State Park, making it a good location for ghost hunting. Sutter's Fort was established in 1841 at a time when most of central California was wild country in the hands of American Indians. John A. Sutter built the place, with thick walls, canons, and heavy gates, as a refuge in the wilderness near the confluence of the American and Sacramento Rivers. After the Bear Flag Revolt of 1846, Sutter's Fort became a hub, an essential stopping point for military units and immigrants entering the new California territory. Hundreds of Indians, Mexicans, and Americans worked at farming, ranching, hunting, and manufacturing goods.

In November 1846, several rescue parties left the fort with supplies for the stranded Donner party, caught in heavy snows in the Sierra. In March and April of 1847, several survivors arrived at the fort and found refuge from their terrible ordeal. Two years later, Sutter and his sawmill operator, James Marshall, discovered gold that led to the great California gold rush of 1849. This event opened the gates of California to hundreds of thousands of gold seekers from all over the world, many of whom rested and re-supplied at Sutter's Fort.

Throughout the 1840s and 1850s, many people died at the fort.

Sutter's Fort, in Sacramento, was built in 1841 and served as a beckon for weary travelers, trappers and explorers, and survivors of the ill-fated Donner Party.

Some were local Indians and Mexicans, while others were thousands of miles from home, destined to never see family again. Some of these lost souls still reside at Sutter's Fort today as spiritual entities. Percipients report the strongest sensations seem to be outside the walls on the west side.

HOTEL LEGER

8304 Main Street
Mokelumne Hill, CA 95245
(916) 286-1401

At the age of thirty-five, George Leger (pronounced Luh-zhay) left his home in Alsace-Lorraine for California's fabled gold rush country. Accompanied by his seventeen-year-old wife, he arrived in Mokelumne Hill in 1851, purchased a lot on Main Street, and began construction of a grand hotel. In 1854, the Hotel de France opened its doors. This elegant hostelry was dubbed the "Queen of the Mother Lode" and quickly became an oasis for gentile society in a town noted for gunfights, murders, unsavory bars and brothels, and bandits such as Joaquin Murieta.

When the Hotel de France was destroyed by fire in the early 1860s, George Leger was devastated. With steadfast devotion to his dream, he cleared away the rubble and built the Hotel Leger in 1865. George lived in his beautiful hotel, looking after every detail, until he was murdered outside his room in 1881. Even death could not separate him from his beloved hotel. Leger's ghost has made it clear that he continues to take a strong interest in the place.

New employees are tested with pranks and nerve-racking ghostly phenomena. Locked doors are found open, and open doors are slammed shut and locked. Tools and equipment have been moved and lights turned on and off. One workman witnessed a window fly open, drawers in a dresser open and close, and a Bible float across a room. Visitors have heard snoring coming from an empty bed, creaking floorboards in empty hallways, and seen the full apparition of George Leger.

One of the hotel's former owners frequently experienced George's presence. Working alone in her office late at night, she felt more secure with the ghost around and thought of him as a guardian angel. She even enjoyed his bizarre antics that included the sudden appearance and disappearance of a yellow balloon tied to the banister. Ghostly activity in George's room—number seven—has been reported by several hotel staff and visitors. The empty rocking chair moves as if George is there, watching the hotel's guests, and the door slams shut if left open too long. Rumpled bed sheets appear as if someone slept in the empty bed.

There may be other ghosts visiting the Hotel Leger. A mysterious woman has been seen on the stairs.

Sighting Report Form

Photocopy and enlarge the form on the next page to a standard 8.5 x 11 inch format. This form should be completed right after a sighting. If the ghost hunt is performed by a group, a designated leader should assume the role of reporter. The reporter is responsible for completing this form.

The reporter and each witness should make a statement, either audio or written, describing in full their experience at the site. Date, sign, and label these statements with a reference number identical to the report number of the sighting report form. Attach the statements to the report form.

SIGHTING REPORT

SITE NAME _____ REPORT #_____
LOCATION _____ DATE: _____
_____ TIME: _____
REPORTER _____ SITE # _____
WITNESSES _____
_____

DESCRIPTION OF APPARITION: _____

temperature change	[] YES	[] NO
auditory phenomena	[] YES	[] NO
telekinesis	[] YES	[] NO
visual phenomena	[] YES	[] NO
other phenomena	[] YES	[] NO

Description: _____

Use the reverse side for diagrams, maps, and drawings.

SPECIFIC LOCATION WITHIN SITE: _____

PREVIOUS SIGHTINGS AT THIS SITE?
          [] YES   [] NO
Reference:

Summary:

RECORDS:
audio   [] YES   [] NO Ref. No. _____
video   [] YES   [] NO Ref. No. _____
photo   [] YES   [] NO Ref. No. _____
Summary of Records _____

Disposition of records: _____

WITNESS STATEMENTS—Summary: _____

witnesses	[] YES	[] NO _____
audio	[] YES	[] NO _____
written	[] YES	[] NO _____

Disposition of statements: _____

APPENDIX B

Suggested Reading

BOOKS

Anderson, Jean. *The Haunting of America.* Boston: Houghton-Mifflin, 1973.

Auerbach, Lloyd. *ESP, Hauntings, and Poltergeists.* New York: Warner Books, 1986.

Bayless, Raymond. *Apparitions and Survival After Death.* New Hyde Park, NY: University Books, 1973.

Beckett, John. *World's Weirest True Ghost Stories.* New York: Sterling Publishing, 1992.

Bradley, Nancy and Vincent Gaddis. *Gold Rush Ghosts.* Garberville, CA: Borderland Sciences Research Foundation, Inc, 1990.

Brown, Sylvia. *Adventures of a Psychic.* New York: Penguin Books, 1990.

Cohen, Daniel. *The Encyclopedia of Ghosts.* New York: Dodd, Mead, 1984.

Ebon, Martin, ed. *The Signet Handbook of Parapsychology.* New York: New American Library, 1978.

Editors of Time-Life Books. *Hauntings.* Alexandria: Time-Life Books, 1991.

Editors of Time-Life Books. *Phantom Encounters.* Alexandria: Time-Life Books, 1991.

Finucane, R.C. *Appearances of the Dead: A Cultural History of Ghosts.* Buffalo: Prometheus Books, 1984.

Haining, Peter. *A Dictionary of Ghost Lore.* Englewood Cliffs, NJ: Prentice-Hall, 1984.

Holzer, Hans. *America's Haunted Houses.* Stanford: Longmeadow Press, 1991.

—-. *Real Hauntings.* New York: Barnes and Noble, 1995.

MacKenzie, Andrew. *Hauntings and Apparitions.* London: Granada Publishing, 1982.

Marinacci, Mike. *Mysterious California.* Los Angeles: Panpipes Press,1988.

May, Antoinette. *Haunted Houses of California.* San Carlos, CA: World Wide Publishing, 1990.

Myers, Arthur. *The Ghostly Register.* Chicago: Contemporary Books, 1986.

Moody, Raymond. *Life after Life.* Atlanta: Mockingbird Books, 1975.

Price, Harry. *Confessions of a Ghost Hunter.* New York: Causeway Books, 1974.

Reinstedt, Randall. *Ghost Tales and Mysterious Happenings of Old Monterey.* Carmel, CA: Ghost Town Publications, 1977.

—-. *Ghostly Tales of Old Monterey.* Carmel, CA: Ghost Town Publications, 1991.

Rogo, Scott. *Mind Beyond the Body.* New York: Penguin Books, 1978.

—-. *An Experience of Phantoms.* New York: Penguin Books, 1974.

Shephard, Leslie A., ed. *Encyclopedia of Occultism and Parapsychology.* Detroit: Gale Research, 1984.

Tanous, Alex, and Harvey Ardman. *Beyond Coincidence: One Man's Experience with Psychic Phenomenon.* Garden City, NY: Doubleday, 1976.

Tyrell, G.N.M. *Apparitions.* New York: Collier Books, 1963.

Underwood, Peter. *The Ghost Hunter's Guide.* Poole, England: Blandford Press, 1986.

Warren, Ed, and Lorraine Warren. *Ghost Hunters.* New York: St. Martin's Press, 1989.

Whitton, Joel, and Joe Fisher. *Life between Life.* New York: Warner Books, 1986.

ARTICLES

Associated Press. "Gone but Not Forgotten." Fairfield (Calif.) Daily Republic, 12 Oct. 1997, sec. B, p.1.

Asche, Jennifer. "Greetings from Santa Creepy: In and Around Santa Cruz, Ghost Stories and Spooky Sites Send Chills Up Visitors' Spines." *San Francisco Chronicle,* October 31, 1997.

Allen-Taylor, J. Douglas. "Ghosts in Our Machines." *Metro: Silicon Valley's Weekly Newspaper,* Oct 28-Nov 3, 1999.

"Borden House Exudes Allure of Macabre." *San Jose Mercury News,* October 15, 1995.

Cianci, Maria. "Clift House Still Charms Dinner Guests and Ghosts: Restaurant Weathers Change on Coastal Perch." *San Francisco Chronicle,* April 14, 1999.

Cochran, Tracy. "The Real Ghost-busters." *Omni Magazine,* August 1988.

Collins, Denis"Under Cover of Darkness California Dreamin' Turns to Nightmare." *San Jose Mercury News,* October 31, 1986.

Cristallo, Suzanne. "Ghost Story." *Los Gatos (Calif.) Weekly Times,* October 27, 1999.

Cristallo, Suzanne. "Bella Saratoga Serves Up Food and History: there's even a friendly ghost." *Saratoga (Calif.) News,* April 1998.

Cromwell, Clarence, and Cecily Barnes. "Restless Spirits: Ghosts Happily Haunt Saratoga and Los Gatos." *Saratoga (Calif.) News,* October 30, 1996.

Cromwell, Clarence. "Restless sirits: Ghosts happily haunt the Hills and Halls of Los Gatos and Saratoga." *Los Gatos (Calif.) Weekly Times,* October 30, 1996.

Dingler, Nancy. "Rockville Park—site of a massacre in 1810." *Daily Republic Fairfield (Calif.),* Sept 24, 2000, sec. C, p. 2.

Evans, Melissa. "Not the usual haunts: tour focuses on the spirits, legends, and lore of Concord." *Massachusetts Sun,* Oct 21, 2000.

Farrell, Brenda. "Haunted hotels deliver temporary chills." *San Jose Mercury News,* Oct 29, 2000.

"Ghosts of Gettysburg: Bones of Civil War Soldier Washed up in Rain Tell a Story to Forensic Scientists." Mercury News Wire Service, *San Jose Mercury News,* December 1, 1996.

"Go from Boom to Bust Through Nevada Ghost Towns." *Contra Costa Times,* September 1,1996.

Hastings, Arthur C. "The Oakland Poltergeist," *Journal of the American Society for Psychical Research,* July 1978.

Heredia, Christopher. "Hometown Haunts: To the Dismay of Some and the Delight of Others, Ghost Stories Never Die." *San Francisco Chronicle,* October 31, 1997.

Hill, Angela. "Paranormal Experts Say it's Not All Funny Business." *Oakland Tribune,* October 18, 2002.

Hogan, Mary Ann. "Who You Gonna Call? Real Ghostbusters." *Oakland Tribune,* September 4, 1984.

"Lady in Grey Starring in Paper's Ghostly Web Site." Mercury News Wire Service. *San Jose Mercury News,* October 31, 1999.

Leary, Kevin. Hotel with invisible guests. *San Francisco Chronicle,* October 31, 1987, sec. A, p. 2.

Marino, Vivian. "A Haunted House can be Tricky to Sell or a Real Treat to Own." *Contra Costa Times* October 29, 1995.

Marshall, Scott. "Barn Houses History: The J.W. Kottinger barn in Pleasanton, built in 1852, was the first jail in Alameda County." *San Ramon Valley (Calif.) Times,* Oct 26, 2000.

Massingill, T. "Business of ghost busting." *Contra Costa Times,* October 8, 2000, sec. D, p. 5.

McCleary, Ingrid. "George—Our Very Own Casper." *Sunnyvale(Calif.) Sun,* November 6, 1996.

McCockran, Robert. "Who Will Tend Graves After M.I. Shuts Down?" *Vallejo (Calif.) Times-Herald,* December 27, 1995.

McManis, Sam. "The X-files of Contra Costa: Paranormal Investigator Lloyd Auerback Shares Tales from the Dark Side." *San Francisco Chronicle,* October 30, 1998.

Nolte, Carl. "A Sport Where the Past is a Presence: Spirits Seem to Linger Near 'The Parting of the Ways.'" *San Francisco Chronicle,* October 20, 1998.

"On the Ghost Watch." Mercury News Wire Service. *San Jose Mercury News,* April 28, 1996.

"Queen Mary: A Favorite Haunt." Mercury News Wire Service. *San Jose Mercury News,* April 4, 1988.

Ramsey, Jane. "Hall leaves legacy of memories." *Brentwood News,* Oct 27, 2000.

Schatzman, Morton. "Living with Apparitions," *New York Times Magazine,* April 27, 1980.

Sens, Josh. "The Truth is Out There—Somewhere." *(San Francisco) Via,* May/June 2002

Spicuzza, Mary. "Urban Legends." *Metro Santa Cruz,* September 22-29, 1999.

Templeton, David. "Ghost Stories: Everyone Knows One." *Sonoma Independent,* June 13-19, 1996.

—-"The Haunted Winery." *Sonoma Independent,* June 13-19, 1996.

Thompson, Ian. "Tracking things that go bump in the night." *Daily Republic,* Oct 29, 2000.

"Tourists Seek Out Chicago's Ghost." Mercury News Wire Service. *San Jose Mercury News,* October 27, 1987.

Appendix C

Films and Videos

Fictional films may provide you with information that will assist you in preparing yourself for a ghost hunt. This assistance ranges from putting you in the proper mood for ghost hunting to useful techniques for exploring haunted places and information about the nature of ghostly activity.

The Amityville Horror (1979). Directed by Stuart Rosenberg. Starring James Brolin and Margot Kidder.

The Canterville Ghost (1996; made for TV). Directed by Sydney Macartney. Starring Patrick Stewart.

Carrie (1976). Directed by Brian De Palma. Starring Sissy Spacek and Piper Laurie.

Cemetery Man (1994). Directed by Michele Soavi. Starring Rupert Everett and Francois Hadji-Lazaro.

City of Angels (1998). Directed by Brad Silberling. Starring Nicolas Cage and Meg Ryan. This is not a "ghost" movie, but excellent portrayal of the ways non-living spirits blend in with life on our plane of existence.

Dragonfly (2002). Directed by Tom Shadyac. Starring Kevin Costner and Kathy Bates. Portrays a dead wife's attempts to communicate with her husband who is an emergency room physician.

The Entity (1983). Directed by Sidney J. Furie. Starring Barbara Hershey and Ron Silver.

Ghost of Flight 409 (1987; made for TV). Directed by Seven Hilliard Stern. Starring Ernest Borgnine and Kim Bassinger. A true story, accurately depicting the appearances of a ghost on board airliners.

Ghost (1990). Directed by Jerry Zucker. Starring Patrick Swayze and Demi Moore.

A contemporary story that clearly depicts the interaction of ghosts with our physical world.

Ghost Story (1981). Directed by John Irvin. Starring Fred Astaire and Melvyn Douglas. Excellent presentation of ghostly phenomena with a bit of horror.

Haunted (1995). Directed by Lewis Gilbert. Starring Aidan Quinn and Kate Beckinsale.

Haunted History. History Channel Home Video. Documentary.

Haunted History of Halloween. History Channel Home Video. Documentary.

Haunted Houses. A & E Home Video. Documentary.

Haunting (1999). Directed by Jan De Bont. Starring Liam Neeson and Catherine-Zeta Jones.

Haunting of Hell House (1999). Directed by Mitch Marcus. Starring Michael York and Claudia Christian.

Haunting of Julia (1976). Directed by Richard Loncraine. Starring Mia Farrow and Keir Dullea.

Haunting of Morella (1991). Directed by Jim Wynorski. Starring David McCallum and Nicole Eggert.

Haunting of Sarah Hardy (1989). Directed by Jerry London. Starring Sela Ward, Michael Woods, and Morgan Fairchild.

Haunting of Seacliff Inn (1995). Directed by Walter Klenhard. Starring Ally Sheedy and William R. Moses. This is one of the best "haunting" films ever made. It highlights the role of unfinished business as a basis for ghostly activity and interaction with the living.

Heartland Ghost (2002). Directed by Brian Trenchard-Smith. Starring Randy Birch and Beau Bridges. Based on a factual about a haunted house in Kansas featured on the reality television series, *Sightings.*

Lady in White (1988). Directed by Frank LaLoggia. Starring Lukas Haas and Len Cariou.

The Others (2001). Directed by Alejandro Amenabar. Starring Nicole Kidman and Christopher Eccleston.

Poltergeist (1982). Directed by Tobe Hooper. Starring JoBeth Williams and Craig T. Nelson.

Poltergeist II: The Other Side (1986). Directed by Brian Gibson. Starring JoBeth Williams and Craig T. Nelson.

Poltergeist III (1988). Directed by Gary Sherman. Starring Tom Skerritt and Nancy Allen.

Restless Spirits (1999). Directed by David Wellington. Starring Lothaire Bluteau, Michel Monty, and Marsha Mason.

Rosemary's Baby (1968). Directed by Roman Polanski. Starring Mia Farrow and John Cassavetes.

Sightings: Ghost Reports (1998). By the producers of the television show *Sightings*. This documentary explores haunted places in the United States with an a team of professional ghost hunters and parapsychologists.

The Sixth Sense (1999). Directed by M. Night Shyamalan. Starring Bruce Willis and Haley Joel Osment. A dead psychologist helps a boy cope with the many ghosts he sees.

The Unexplained: Hauntings. A & E Home Video.

SPECIAL TOURS AND ACTIVITIES

Winchester Mystery House. Candle-light tours on Halloween and special Friday the 13th events. 525 South Winchester Boulevard, San Jose, CA 95128-2537. Call (408) 247-2000.

Halloween Dinner and Revelry. The Vineyard House, PO Box 176, 530 Cold Springs Road, Colma, CA 95613. Call (916) 622-2217.

American Society for Psychical Research list of Courses and Other Study Opportunities in Parapsychology. ASPR, 5 West Seventy-Third Street, New York, NY 10023. Call (212) 799-5050.

Constitution Days. A weekend celebration of the Gold Rush days in an authentic gold rush town. Visitors and locals dress in period clothing and mingle with ghosts of a bygone era. Scheduled for the weekend following Labor Day. Nevada City, CA. Contact Nevada City Visitor's Bureau.

Doc Ricketts Birthday Celebration. The lab is open for public tours only three times per year on Steinbeck's birthday (February 27), during the annual Sardine Festival (early June), and on Doc Ricketts' birthday (May 14). Cannery Row, Monterey. Call the Cannery Row Foundation at (831) 372-8512.

Jack London Birthday Celebration. The celebration of the birth of the celebrated author in January 12, 1876. The dinner party is held on the Saturday closest to this date. Boyes' Hot Springs Golf Club on Arnold Drive between Sonoma and Glen Ellen. Call the Jack London Bookstore at (707) 996-2888.

International Society for Paranormal Research conducts ghost expeditions and tours of haunted places in the U.S. and in Europe. ISPR, 4712 Admiralty Way, Marina Del Rey, CA 90292.

Ghost Towns Guided Tours of Arizona. Call (602) 273-6308. Web site: www.ghosttowns.com.

Renstorff House Tours. Tours and rental of the 1867 Victorian mansion are available. Shoreline Park, Mountain View, CA 94040. Call (650) 903-6088 or 961-5321.

Potomac cruises. Come cruise on the presidential yacht. 540 Water Street (PO Box 2064), Oakland, CA 94604. Call the office at (510) 627-1215 or the twenty-four hour information line at (510) 839-8256.

City of Clayton Ghost Walk. Every Halloween locals and visitors gather to stroll the streets of Clayton stopping at several haunted sites. Call the Clayton Historical Society at (925) 672-0240.

Tours of Alcatraz by day or night. Stand in a cell formerly occupied by world-famous criminals. Take a walk on death row. This is a spooky place by day and scarier by night. Private events can be arranged with the National Park Service. Web site: www.nps.gov/Alcatraz/.

San Francisco's Barbary Coast Trail. The San Francisco Museum and Historical Society sponsors this 3.8-mile tour that connects twenty fascinating sites including one of the largest collection of historic ships in the U.S. Web site: www.sfhistory.org

Black Diamond Mines Regional Preserve. The East Bay Regional Parks District offers an underground tour of the Hazel-Atlas mine. This mine is adjacent to the remains of three 1860s coal-mining towns, including Nortonville and its cemetery Call (925) 757-2620. Web site: www.ebparks.org.

San Francisco Ghost Hunt Walking Tours. Visit several sites of documented ghostly activity. SF Ghost Tours, 764 North Pont #12, San Francisco, CA 94109. Call (415) 922-5590.

Organizations

American Society for Psychical Research
5 West Seventy-Third Street
New York, New York 10023
(212) 799-5050

Astrological and Psychical Society
124 Trefoilo Crescent
Broadfeld, Crawley
West Sussex RH119EZ
England

Bay Area Skeptics
P.O. Box 60
Concord, CA 94522

Berkeley Psychic Institute
2436 Hastings Street
Berkeley, CA 94704
(510) 548-8020

British Society for Psychical Research
Eleanor O'Keffe, secretary
49 Marloes Road
London W86LA
England
44-71-937-8984

Center for Applied Intuition
2046 Clement Street
San Francisco, CA 94121

Central Premonitions Registry
P.O. Box 482
Times Square Station
New York, NY 10036

Center for Scientific Anomalies Research
P.O. Box 1052
Ann Arbor, Michigan 48103

Committee for Scientific Investigations of Claims of the Paranormal
1203 Kensington Avenue
Buffalo, NY 14215

Stanford University
Department of Psychology
Jordan Hall, Building 420
Stanford, CA 94305

Division of Parapsychology
Box 152, Medical Center
Charlottesville, VA 22908

Graduate Parapsychology Program
John F. Kennedy University
12 Altarinda Road
Orinda, CA 94563
(415) 254-0200

Institute for Noetic Sciences
2658 Bridgewood Drive
Sausalito, CA 94965

Institute for Parapsychology
Box 6847
College Station
Durham, NC 27708

International Society for Paranormal Research
4712 Admiralty Way
Marina del Rey, CA 90292

International Ghost Hunter's Organization
www.ghostweb.com/index.html

Haunted Valley Paranormal
www.hauntedvalley.4mg.com/

Parapsychology Foundation
228 East Seventy-First Street
New York, NY 10021
(212) 628-1550

Parapsychology Research group
3101 Washington Street
San Francisco, CA 94115

Psi Applications
Steve Moreno
Fairfield, CA 94533 (no mailing address)
(707) 425-4382

Psychical Research Foundation
C/o William Roll
Psychology Department
West Georgia College
Carrolton, GA 30118

Saybrook Institute
1772 Vallejo Street
San Francisco, CA 94109

Spiritual Emergency Network
California Institute of Transpersonal Psychology
250 Oak Grove Avenue
Menlo Park, CA 94025
(510) 327-2776

Society for Psychical Research
1 Adam and Eve Mewes
Kensington, W8 6UG
England

Southern California Society for Psychical Research
269 South Arden Boulevard
Los Angeles, CA 90004

Internet Sources

www.theshadowlands.net/ghost. This Web site lists thousands of haunted sites.

www.london-ghost-walk.co.UK. Information on a tour through London's haunted streets.

www.hauntings.com. Web site for the International Society for Paranormal Research.

www.historichotels.nationaltrust.org. Historic hotels of America are detailed here.

www.paranormal.com. This Web site has a live chat room and links to news articles about paranormal activities.

www.ghoststalkers.com. This is the Web site of Terry L. Smith and Mark Jean, who call themselves the "Ghost Stalkers."

www.ghostweb.com/. Web site of the International Ghost Hunters Society.

www.ghosttowns.com. Informative Web site that gives detailed information about ghost towns in the United States and Canada.

www.ghostbusters.com. The official Web site of the movie *Ghostbusters*.

www.parapsychology.com. Links to several relative Web sites.

www.psi-app.com. PSI is dedicated to the investigation and documentation of anomalous events, including paranormal.

www.hgtv.com. Click on "ghostcam" to see real-time view of a haunted place.

www.historychannel.com. The official Web site of the History Channel.

www.winchestermysteryhouse.com. Information about the Winchester Mystery House of San Jose.

www.mysteryspot.com. Information about the Mystery Spot of Santa Cruz Mountains.

www.californiahistory.org. This site links with State Historic Parks.

www.sfhistory.org. San Francisco Museum and Historical Society Web site.

www.nps.gov. National Park Service; locations include many historic sites.

www.rightondesign.com/baprs/index.htlm. Web site of the Bar Area Paranormal Research Society.

www.hauntedvalley.4mg.com/. Tri-Valley Research Team investigates paranormal activity in the Livermore area.

www.yahoo.com. For maps and driving instructions to a site Click on "maps." Enter your address (or any starting point), then enter the address of the haunted place you wish to visit. Yahoo will generate a free map and driving instructions including an estimate of driving time and total miles.

Historical Societies and Museums

Historical societies and museums are good places to discover information about old houses and other buildings or places that figure prominently in local history. They often contain records, in the form of old newspapers and diaries, about tragic events such as fires, hangings, train wrecks, and earthquakes that led to the loss of life. Old photographs and maps may be available to serious researchers that are not on display for public viewing. Some of these organizations have Web sites that offer access to rare photographs, maps, and other research material.

Alameda Historical Society
2324 Alameda Avenue
Alameda, CA 94501
(510) 521-1233

Belmont Historical Society
1219 Ralston Avenue
Belmont, CA 94002
(650) 593-4213
www.belmont.gov.orgs/BHS/

Benicia Historical Society
PO Box 773
Vallejo, CA 94590
(707) 745-1822

Berkeley Historical Society
931 Center Street
Berkeley, CA 94704
(510) 848-0181
www.ci.berkeley.ca.us/histsoc/

Bodega Bay Historical Society
1580 Eastshore Road
Bodega Bay, CA 94923
(707) 875-9255

Burlingame Historical Society
900 Burlingame Avenue
Burlingame, CA 94010
(650) 340-9960
www.burlingamehistorical.org

California History Center
21250 Stevens Creek Boulevard
Cupertino, CA 95014
(408) 864-8712

California Historical Society
687 Mission Street
San Francisco, CA 94105
(415) 357-1848

Campbell Historical Museum
51 North Central Avenue
Campbell, CA 95008
(408) 866-2119

Chinese Historical Society
965 Clay Street
San Francisco, CA 94108
(415) 391-1188
www.chsa.org

Clayton Historical Society
6101 Main Street
Clayton, CA 94517
(925) 672-0240
www.claytonHS.com/

Colma History Guild Museum
40 Wembley Drive
Daly City, CA 94105
(650) 755-5123

Concord Historical Society
1601 Sutter Street #EF
Concord, CA 94520
(925) 827-3380
www.conhistsoc.org

Concord Family History Center
3700 Concord Boulevard
Concord, CA 94519
(925) 686-1766

Crockett Historical Museum
900 Loring Avenue
Crockett, CA 94525
(510) 787-2178

Fremont Museum of Local History
190 Anza Street
Fremont, CA 94539
(510) 623-7907
www.museumoflocalhistory.org

Hayward Historical Society
22701 Main Street
Hayward, CA 94541
(510) 581-0223
www.haywardareahistory.org

Los Gatos History Club
123 Los Gatos Boulevard
Los Gatos, CA 95030
(408) 354-9825

Marin County Historical Society
1125 B Street
San Rafael, CA 94901
(415) 454-8538
www.marinhistory.org

Menlo Park Historical Society
800 Alma Street
Menlo Park, CA 94025
(650) 858-3368

Monterey County Historical
   Society
333 Boronda Road
Salinas, CA 93907
(831) 757-8085
www.mchsmuseum.com

Napa County Historical Society
1219 First Street
Napa, CA 94559
(707) 224-1739
www.mapahistory.org/contact.html

Oakland Museum
1000 Oak Street
Oakland, CA 94611
(510) 238-2200

Pacific Grove Heritage Society
605 Laurel Avenue
Pacific Grove, CA 93950
(831) 372-2898
www.mabay.net/~heritage/

Palo Alto Historical Association
PO Box 193
Palo Alto, CA 94302
(650) 326-3355
www.pahistory.org/

Petaluma Historical Museum
20 Fourth Street
Petaluma, CA 94954
(707) 778-4398

Pittsburg Historical Society
515 Railroad Avenue
Pittsburg, CA 94565
(925) 439-7501

Presidential Yacht Potomac
540 Water Street
Oakland, CA 94607
(510) 839-7533
www.usspotomac.org/

Presido Historical Association
Presido of San Francisco
San Francisco, CA 94129
(415) 921-8193

Richmond Museum of History
400 Nevin Avenue
Richmond, CA 94801
(510) 235-7387

Saratoga Historical Museum
20450 Saratoga-Los Gatos Road
Saratoga, CA 95070
(408) 867-4311

San Jose Historical Museum
1300 Senter Road
San Jose, CA 95112
(408) 277-2757

San Mateo County History
  Museum
777 Hamilton Street
Redwood City, CA 94063
(650) 299-0104
www.sanmateocountyhistory.com

Santa Clara Valley Historical
  Society
580 College Avenue
Palo Alto, CA 94306
(650) 857-0765

Sausalito Historical Society
420 Litho Street
Sausalito, CA 94965
(415) 289-4117

Tomales Bay Regional History
  Center
26701 Highway 1
Tomales, CA 94971
(707) 878-9443

Tracy Historical Museum
1141 Adams Street
Tracy, CA 95376
(209) 832-7278

Vallejo Naval History Museum
734 Marin Street
Vallejo, CA 94590
(707) 643-0077
www.vallejomuseum.org

Western Aerospace Museum
  (Oakland Airport)
8260 Boeing Street
Oakland, CA 94621
(510) 638-7100

Wells Fargo History Museum
420 Montgomery Street
San Francisco, CA 94104
(415) 396-2619

Index